C000259943

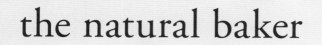

the natural baker

the natural baker

a new way to bake using the best natural ingredients

Henrietta Inman

jacqui
small

Design, layout and photography copyright © 2018
Quarto Publishing Group plc
Text copyright © 2018 Henrietta Inman

First published in 2018 by
Jacqui Small
An imprint of The Quarto Group
The Old Brewery
6 Blundell Street
London N7 9BH
T (0)20 7700 6700 **F** (0)20 7700 8066

The author's moral rights have been asserted.

Publisher: Jacqui Small
Senior Commissioning Editor: Fritha Saunders
Managing Editor: Emma Heyworth-Dunn
Senior Designer: Rachel Cross
Photographer: Philippa Langley
Editor: Lucy Bannell
Production: Maeve Healy
Food Stylist: Henrietta Inman
Prop Stylists: Linda Berlin and Henrietta Inman
Image between front cover and page 1: Lisa Linder

ISBN: 978 191112 730 7

A catalogue record for this book is available
from the British Library.

2019 2018 2017
10 9 8 7 6 5 4 3 2 1

Printed in China

The cover shows (clockwise from top right):
blackberry, blueberry and hazelnut tart;
caramelized apple and almond tart;
plum and almond tart;
raspberry, fig and pistachio tart.
All are variations of the recipe on page 153.

Quarto is the authority on a wide range of topics.

Quarto educates, entertains and enriches the lives of
our readers – enthusiasts and lovers of hands-on living.

www.QuartoKnows.com

CONTENTS

introduction

I have thought long and hard about how my natural way of baking evolved, and have come to realize that it was my upbringing in the Suffolk countryside that stands out as the greatest influence. Though I now live in London, I often return to Suffolk and it never ceases to inspire my work. Surrounded by fields of grains, growing and eating fruits and vegetables from our garden, local free-range eggs, dairy, meat and fish, I was able to understand from a young age where food came from, and I also learned to appreciate the quality of simple wholefoods. Learning how to cook with these ingredients has shaped the way I eat today, as well as my style of baking... well, that and a bit of a sweet tooth!

As a keen artist, everything I bake just has to look beautiful, too. After all, we eat with our eyes first. When I lived in France and Italy as part of my degree, I tasted for the first time the great delights of *pâtisserie* and *pasticceria*. So, at 21, I enrolled on a pâtisserie scholarship, trained as an apprentice and went on to work in award-winning hotels and restaurants. After five years in London, I hankered after the countryside, so I moved home to Suffolk. I started a business selling what I baked at farmers' markets, shops and pop-ups, teaching and making cakes to order. And, quite suddenly and unexpectedly, over a very short time, my baking took me in a new direction.

Back in the countryside again, I wanted to get all those wonderful ingredients with which I had grown up into my baking. I am sure that working very long hours in subterranean city kitchens had something to do with it, too. I was tired and – apart from yearning for sleep – just longed for really good, wholesome and nourishing food. That food made its way into my baking... and what an adventure was to come.

Fortunately, wheat, spelt and rye flours were available locally, as were local oil, butter, yogurt and cheese, not to mention all the vibrantly coloured, flavour-packed fruits and vegetables. I wanted to apply a pâtissière's techniques and skills to baking with more natural – and less traditional – ingredients. As much as I adore classic pâtisserie and its repertoire of sponges, pastries and doughs, I wanted to substitute its plain (all-purpose) flour and caster (superfine) sugar with more wholegrain flours, less-refined sweeteners such as local honey and brown sugars, and less-processed fats such as extra virgin cold-pressed rapeseed (canola) oil.

At the same time, many of my customers were asking for gluten- and dairy-free items, wanted to know how to bake them and, most importantly, how to make them taste good, complaining that so many of the alternatives on offer were unfulfilling in texture and flavour. This led me to other discoveries, of delicious, naturally gluten-free flours such as wholegrain buckwheat, quinoa, teff and brown rice, and to using more oats in my baking, as well as nut flours such as chestnut and almond. I also discovered virgin coconut oil and nut and seed butters and pastes. The wholegrain flours were nutty; the sugars richer and with caramel notes; the rapeseed (canola) oil had an earthy flavour while the coconut oil was lighter with a hint of vanilla.

I made these tasty grains, sweeteners and fats my core ingredients, then layered on to them the stand-out flavours of dark chocolate, citrus, spices, nuts, seeds, dried fruits and zingy fresh fruits, which I call my magic ingredients. At once, my cakes, biscuits (cookies), tarts, breads – indeed everything I baked – took on an excitingly new and interesting flavour dimension.

This book is a celebration of the vast array and diversity of all those natural ingredients, with recipes to help you become a natural baker in your own home. Eating well is so important for keeping us healthy and happy, and cooking fresh food from scratch, made with proper ingredients, will do just that. A bit of balance and variety are important, too, with many of us choosing lighter dishes during the week and allowing for a little bit more indulgence on some evenings and at weekends. There are all types of these recipes in this book, as well as simpler bakes for busy weekdays, or slightly more challenging projects for when you have more time to spare… and many more. The ingredients are affordable and easy to find and the recipes are accessible and inviting.

Natural ingredients, for me, are simply those without additives, preservatives or colourings. They have been interfered with as little as possible between harvest and reaching the kitchen, such as wholegrain flours, less-refined cane and coconut sugars, other sweeteners such as raw honey and maple syrup, and real fats and oils. I also embrace products sourced seasonally and locally whenever possible. I believe that there are no other ingredients with more flavours or interesting textures than these natural foods, and so it simply makes the most sense to me to use them in my baking.

A quick note about how I put the book together and how to use it to best serve your baking. The chapter divisions are just a guide: there might be a recipe in Breakfasts that you feel like having for lunch, or even a dish from Desserts & Puddings that gives leftovers that you might enjoy for breakfast. And feel free to be creative: when I cook from a book, I follow a recipe the first time I make it; when I make it the second time, I can then adapt it to my tastes, if necessary, depending on the ingredients I have in my cupboard, what is in season, or if I am cooking for anyone with a special dietary requirement. I hope that you will do the same, and make these recipes your own. At the beginning of each chapter, you'll find more about the recipes to come, the ingredients used, and how and why I combine them in the ways that I do.

By balancing the flavour, quality and texture of classic pâtisserie with the fullness, value and goodness of simple wholefoods, I have created recipes that are delicious, exciting and unique, to satisfy and sustain you and make you smile. Wholefood recipes that really do taste wonderful.

Good food can bring so much happiness in so many ways. I hope that baking these recipes will bring as much joy to you as creating them has brought to me.

CORE INGREDIENTS

Most baking recipes are built from four main ingredients: a flour, a sweetener, some kind of fat, and eggs. To these, a small amount of raising agent is often added, perhaps a little salt, too. I call these the 'core ingredients', as they are the building blocks of my baking. I go into some depth about their flavours and textures here, and you'll find more information throughout the book. As you get to know these ingredients, I hope you enjoy finding the most delicious ways to combine them as much as I do.

FLOURS

These add bulk, structure and texture to recipes. I like to use mainly wholegrain flours, because of the unique tastes and richness they contribute to my baking. When a bit of lightness of crumb is required, or more delicate flavours are to be added, I use white flour, either on its own or combined with a wholegrain version. Wheat and spelt flours – more often in their wholegrain form but sometimes in their white or strong form – and wholegrain rye flour, sometimes dark, are the main flours I use, as they are reliable, creating good results with great taste and texture. They are also grown in the UK. Rye is lower in gluten than wheat and spelt, so less powerful for binding and rising.

I occasionally use einkorn and emmer, two ancient varieties of wheat (as is spelt), and barley flour, a grain grown in the UK, for their rich tastes. Sometimes I combine them with rye and common wheat; in general, combining flours creates unique texture and increased depth of flavour.

Wholegrain buckwheat flour, brown rice flour, brown teff flour, oat flour and polenta (cornmeal) – as with all the ingredients I select – are chosen first and foremost because of their unique and varying tastes and textures. It is a bonus that they are also naturally gluten-free, so great for those with allergies. Quinoa and millet, also gluten-free, are fabulous in their wholegrain forms, adding nubbly crunch, whether mixed into bread doughs, or combined with vegetables in savoury baked dishes. Yellow pea flour and chickpea (garbanzo bean) flour are great in savoury breads and pancakes, with moreish, distinct and warming tastes; while ground almonds, other ground nuts and chestnut flour create delicious moist cakes and are great in biscuits (cookies) and pastry, giving a good crumb. (And all of these are, incidentally, naturally gluten-free.)

SWEET THINGS

These add bulk, give a good consistency and, most importantly, enhance and complement other flavours with their uplifting sweetness. Use your judgement: if in doubt, always add less sweetener, as you can always serve a cake or dessert with a drizzle of honey or maple syrup or a bowl of sugar.

The granulated sweeteners I use most are coconut sugar or light brown muscovado sugar, both with a delicious caramel-toffee taste. Though I love to use the former, it is expensive and can be hard to find. Therefore, the majority of the recipes have been created so you can choose which you want to use. Dark brown muscovado sugar and liquid molasses are richer, with more treacly notes. All these four stand up well to robust ingredients.

To flatter delicate flavours – lavender, for example – I use lighter golden caster (superfine) and golden icing (confectioners') sugar. As for liquid sweeteners, I use honey, local whenever possible and – if I can – raw, as it is less processed; also maple and date syrup; the former is lighter in taste.

FATS

Fats and oils add a softness to baked goods, as well as moisture and a rich taste. In pastry and biscuits (cookies), they give a crumbly quality. Unsalted butter creamed with sugar creates light sponges and flaky pastries. Extra virgin cold-pressed rapeseed (canola) oil, extra virgin olive oil and virgin coconut oil all have their uses and unique flavours; they are also dairy-free, vital for those with allergies. Replace cow's dairy products with those made from goat's and sheep's milk if necessary.

EGGS, RAISING AGENTS & SALT

Eggs add rise, lightness, a lot of moisture and help to bind ingredients. (Though I sometimes use milled flaxseeds mixed with water as a binder and egg replacement, see page 82.)

Raising agents are important in cakes, muffins and quick breads, creating good rise and lightness. Bicarbonate of soda (baking soda) is an alkaline. To create rise, it needs to react with an acid such as yogurt, buttermilk or vinegar; this reaction also helps to add a crisp crust. Baking powder is made from alkaline bicarbonate of soda (baking soda) and an acid in the form of solid crystals, commonly cream of tartar, so is a complete leavening agent.

Salt is very important, not just for savoury dishes, but also for lifting flavours in sweet recipes, where just a little is needed. I use sea salt flakes that I crumble between my fingers before adding.

MAGIC INGREDIENTS

These are added to core ingredients, to the sponge, the pastry, the dough, to give those extra 'wow' flavours and textures. The wholegrain flours, natural sweeteners, fats and oils discussed above already bring a lot of flavour to the recipes; that is exactly why I use them! When both the core and magic ingredients have so much flavour and texture, they are all equally the stars of the show.

GRAINS

I love rolled and jumbo oats for their nubbliness; oat bran for a mealy warmth and heft; puffed rice and buckwheat groats for their great crunch; and millet flakes for a gentle bite. All of these add more texture to recipes and show the grains in different forms, not just as flour. Use gluten-free oats, if necessary, which are processed away from gluten.

DRIED FRUIT

Dates, figs, apricots, prunes, raisins, sultanas (golden raisins) and cranberries add natural sweetness and a chewy quality. Dates, figs and prunes have rich tastes, great with wholegrain flours and brown sugars, as well as with dark chocolate and nuts. I love to heat them with water or a citrus juice, to make a sweet paste. Mashed bananas, Apple purée (see page 102) and grated root vegetables all add sweetness and moisture, too.

FRESH PRODUCE

Seasonal fruits and vegetables add insurmountable flavour and colour to my recipes and are probably my favourite magic ingredients. Fresh herbs are also great in both sweet and savoury recipes, as are spices. In sweet recipes, a little cinnamon or vanilla can really boost the other notes. Citrus fruits, their juices and especially their zests are great for this, too, as well as for keeping things fresh-tasting.

DAIRY AND DAIRY-FREE ALTERNATIVES AND MEAT

Whole milk, yogurt, soured cream, crème fraîche, buttermilk (see page 62 for a dairy-free alternative), mascarpone, ricotta, goat's cheese, feta and other cheeses add great tang and create a luscious, soft character. Cream is used whipped as an accompaniment, with chocolate in a ganache, or added to quiche fillings. All dairy produce and meat must be bought fresh; please do try to source it grass-fed, local and / or organic when you can. Raw milk – and cheese and butter made from it – is wonderful. I also love to use unsweetened nut milks for their tastes and as a dairy-free alternative. (Rice and oat milks are available, too, if you avoid nuts.)

NUTS AND SEEDS

These add so much bite and taste. Nut butters and seed pastes are good in doughs, giving a crumbly structure. Desiccated (dried) coconut and coconut flakes are great for crunch, especially toasted flakes.

FLOWERS, FLOWER WATERS, TEA, COFFEE, CHOCOLATE & ALCOHOL

I love to use dried flowers such as lavender, flower waters and teas such as rooibos, as well as fresh edible flowers for finishing touches. These are all delicately flavoured. Cocoa or cacao powder, dark chocolate and coffee are much richer and more robust. Spirits, white and red wine are always good for unctuousness and depth.

GLUTEN- & DAIRY-FREE, VEGAN & VEGETARIAN BAKING

Lots of the recipes in this book are great for those with dietary requirements, or can easily be adapted. For example, remove the cheese, meat or fish in savoury recipes if necessary, or use the water ganache tart filling (see page 144) as a quick dairy-free chocolate icing or spread. Coconut cream can be whipped up as an icing or accompaniment (see page 168), while recipes that call for melted butter can sometimes be replaced with virgin coconut oil, as in teatime soda bread (see page 62), though this is not a literal rule, so experimentation is required. Dairy-free butter is available, milk can be replaced with dairy-free versions, there is coconut yogurt and even a cream made from oats!

For more information on how gluten and dairy function in baking, or for more vegan recipes, please have a look at my first book, *Clean Cakes*.

BAKING TIPS & TECHNIQUES

There are many recurring techniques in this book, and in baking in general. This section is for your reference and to help you with the recipes. When teaching, I often hear students say baking is difficult, but I promise you it is not. I always advise you to read a recipe right to the end before starting, make sure you have the correct ingredients ready, preheat the oven and have a reliable set of electronic scales. With these matters ticked off, you are already halfway there. Follow the key points laid out below, and you will be a master of baking before you know it. I outline the methods in most recipes, too, for your ease and to save time flicking back through pages, but if anything is ever unclear, just come back to these pages.

INGREDIENTS

Unless specified, **flours** are wholegrain. Buy regular wholegrain rye flour, unless dark rye is called for.

All **eggs** are large, unless specified. Make sure that your eggs are at room temperature, so that they do not cause cake mixtures to split. Leftover egg whites can be refrigerated for up to 5 days in a sealed container, frozen for up to 1 month, or made into meringues (see page 172). Leftover egg yolks can be kept in the fridge for up to 5 days in a sealed container: use cling film (plastic wrap) before sealing, touching it to the surface of the yolks so they do not dry out. Use them up in pastry and mayonnaise.

MEASUREMENTS

For precision and ease, liquid measures are given as weights throughout. Millilitres and grams are roughly the same, so 300g water, milk or double (heavy) cream, for example, will be about 300ml.

OVER- & UNDER-MIXING

Make sure that baking powder and bicarbonate of soda (baking soda) are always well dispersed into the rest of the dry ingredients before adding wet ingredients; a whisk is great for this and saves the faff of a sieve. Too much raising agent can cause an acidic, unappealing taste, and cause a cake to rise quickly when baking, then suddenly drop.

Remember that combining techniques can also have an effect on the texture of the final product, so treat batters lightly, folding when necessary and not knocking air out by mixing too roughly. As soon as the components are combined and no more dry ingredients can be seen, stop mixing.

EQUIPMENT

Ovens vary so much, so please bear in mind that cooking times are a guide and should be altered according to the manufacturer's instructions.

All the recipes in the book were tested in a convection fan-assisted oven. In general, conventional ovens may need to be set at 10°C (50°F) hotter (no more) than the printed temperatures, and the bake time could be slightly longer. Always preheat the oven so it reaches the required temperature before baking. For even heat distribution, I place the baking tin (pan) in the middle of the oven and almost always rotate it halfway through baking, as ovens are often hotter at the back, and sometimes on one side, too.

Electronic scales are the most reliable, accurate and straightforward, saving on washing up, especially for weighed liquid measurements. Thanks to the tare button, you can weigh everything into the same bowl. Precisely weighed ingredients are a key part of baking, so I recommend investing in a set. They are reasonably priced and sold in all kitchen and electrical shops.

Metric **measuring spoons** – as opposed to random teaspoons and tablespoons – are so important. All quantities in this book are for level spoons, unless otherwise specified.

Small **step or cranked palette knives** are an incredibly versatile and useful piece of equipment, used to apply icings to cakes, for smoothing out batters in tins (pans) or fillings in pastry shells.

Microplane **graters** are excellent for finely grating citrus zests, while box graters are ideal for vegetables and cheeses for cakes, scones and breads.

Vegetable **peelers** are indispensable for peeling, paring citrus zests and making vegetables such as courgettes (zucchini) and carrots into ribbons.

Sharp knives make work a lot easier. Serrated knives make easy work of slicing items such as tomatoes, bread or brittle granola bars.

Silicone **spatulas** are good for folding and scraping out bowls, making sure all the ingredients are used and that there is no waste.

Balloon whisks disperse ingredients well (see note, left, on over- and under-mixing).

Food processors are great for fine or coarse chopping, especially nuts, using the chopping or 'S'-blade, and for emulsions, quick cake mixes and binding ingredients in certain recipes.

When a recipe calls for a **bain-marie or double boiler**, fit a heatproof bowl – ceramic, Pyrex or aluminium – over a pan of simmering water to melt chocolate and butter. (The bowl should not touch the water.)

A few more things will make your baking easier: **baking parchment**, preferably unbleached; **chopping boards**; **freestanding or hand-held mixer** for easy whisking and mixing with **whisk and paddle attachments**; **hook attachment** for bread dough; **hand-held blender**; selection of **baking tins (pans)**; **saucepans** (I like heavy-based cast iron or stainless steel); Pyrex, glass, ceramic or metal **bowls**.

TINS (PANS)

All tins (pans) were measured around their tops.

When recipes specify greasing the base and sides of a tin (pan), do so with a piece of kitchen paper or a pastry brush, using a thin layer of the fat or oil particular to the recipe. With the kitchen paper or brush, grease in an upward movement, from the bottom up, as if to help the cake rise. I always do this first, so that the baking parchment then sticks, to allow for a cake or loaf to be baked with straight, clean edges. Place the tin (pan) on to a piece of baking parchment, draw around the base with a pencil and then cut it out, to achieve the right size of paper to line the base. Normally only the base of the tin (pan) needs paper, but if a recipe takes longer to cook, such as a fruit cake or banana bread, I often line the edges with paper as well, to stop the sides from darkening too much. To make a collar for cakes that rise a lot, just cut a piece of baking parchment to wrap around the inside circumference of the tin (pan), tall enough to come a good few centimetres (1in) up and over the edges.

PASTRY (PIE DOUGH)

To make your pastry (pie dough) by hand, rub the fat into the flour with your fingertips until the mix resembles crumbs, then add the eggs or other wet ingredients and mix to form the dough. You can also do this using a freestanding mixer fitted with a paddle attachment. Food processors can be used, but I prefer not to, as butter can become soft too quickly, and it is easy to over-work the mixture. Do not make pastry (pie dough) in a blender!

If the pastry dough is warm after making, refrigerate it for 30 minutes. If it is still cool and not too sticky, then roll it between two pieces of lightly floured baking parchment; this stops the dough sticking to the work surface and the rolling pin. When it is 3mm (⅛in) thick, lift off the top piece of parchment, place it back down, flip the pastry and lift off the other piece of parchment, just to be sure the pastry isn't sticking to it.

Remove the top parchment and either flip the dough into your prepared tin (best for gluten-free pastry or rye pastry with its low gluten content), or flour the pastry, then roll it up over the rolling pin, then roll it out over the tin (pan). Push the dough into the corners of the tin (pan), making sure there are no air gaps. Trim with a knife. Refrigerate for 30 minutes or freeze the raw pastry shell for up to 1 month. Bake according to the recipe instructions.

For blind baking – baking a tart shell before it is filled – line the rested pastry with a piece of baking parchment, fill with baking beans, raw rice or dried pulses and bake according to the recipe (see page 138).

When baked, I often brush a layer of egg yolk over the tart shell and return it to the oven for a few minutes to dry it out. This creates a seal between the pastry and filling and keeps the pastry from becoming soggy; it's particularly important for liquid fillings in quiches and custard tarts. For these, another good tip is to place the baked pastry shell in the oven, pull out the oven shelf and pour in the liquid filling from a jug to avoid any spillages.

HOW TO TELL WHEN IT'S READY

This is a rough guide, as all baked products vary, but there are general rules and signs.

Cakes and muffins are ready when a skewer inserted into the centre comes out clean, the top is golden brown and bounces back when touched, and it is coming away from the sides of the tin (pan). However, a skewer inserted into brownies will come out only-just-clean and the top may be cracking.

Biscuits (cookies) and pastry should be golden brown and just firm to the touch.

Bread will sound hollow when tapped on the bottom, with a golden brown, hard-ish crust.

Quiches, custards and baked mousses are ready when they are just set with a little wobble.

Remember, all bakes will carry on cooking a little more once out of the oven.

STORING & FREEZING

I prefer to store cakes in the fridge, especially those that are soft and damp or with fresh dairy icings, moist items such as banana or nut breads, malt loaves and muffins, tarts, quiches and pies. Make sure they are in an airtight container or covered well with cling film (plastic wrap); I put a layer of baking parchment on first, to avoid any plastic taint. When I want them, I let them come to room temperature for the texture to normalize. If this goes against your usual ways of storing and you'd rather stick to those, then please do! (Though remember mould grows faster on moist goods.)

If they are in the fridge, most baked items will keep for at least 5 days; smelling and tasting small amounts to check they are still OK is the best way to avoid waste.

I also note on each recipe what is suitable to freeze (most things are). They can be frozen whole, wrapped as for refrigerated items (see above), or frozen in slices: put slices on a tray lined with baking parchment and freeze. Once frozen solid, place in an airtight container or freezer bag. This way, slices are frozen individually and can be removed easily.

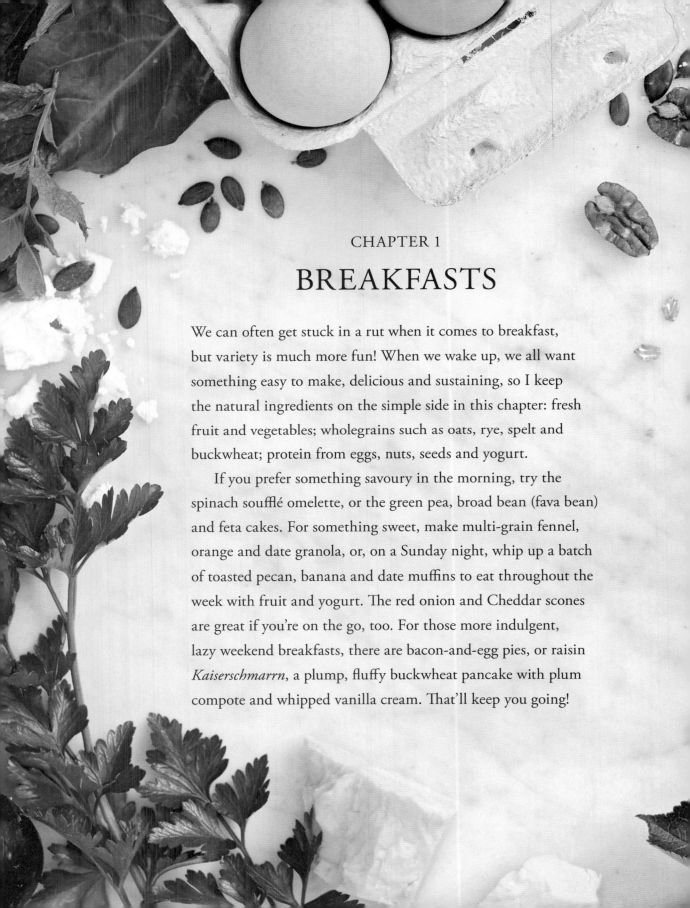

CHAPTER 1

BREAKFASTS

We can often get stuck in a rut when it comes to breakfast, but variety is much more fun! When we wake up, we all want something easy to make, delicious and sustaining, so I keep the natural ingredients on the simple side in this chapter: fresh fruit and vegetables; wholegrains such as oats, rye, spelt and buckwheat; protein from eggs, nuts, seeds and yogurt.

If you prefer something savoury in the morning, try the spinach soufflé omelette, or the green pea, broad bean (fava bean) and feta cakes. For something sweet, make multi-grain fennel, orange and date granola, or, on a Sunday night, whip up a batch of toasted pecan, banana and date muffins to eat throughout the week with fruit and yogurt. The red onion and Cheddar scones are great if you're on the go, too. For those more indulgent, lazy weekend breakfasts, there are bacon-and-egg pies, or raisin *Kaiserschmarrn*, a plump, fluffy buckwheat pancake with plum compote and whipped vanilla cream. That'll keep you going!

Walnut and flaxseed (linseed) banana bread with lots of toppings

We all need a quick banana bread recipe in our repertoire, so I wanted to share mine with you. It's quick to make and nourishing, packed full of fibre and wholesome deliciousness. I love its caramel flavour from the honey and bananas, the soft, sweet vanilla notes from the coconut oil, the crunch from the seeds and the great crust. It's also not too sweet, allowing for extra drizzles of honey or maple syrup once it gets on your plate, if you want. It's a mash-it-up, shove-it-in-the-tin kind of cakey-loaf. Bake it in the evening, ready for breakfast the next morning; when the timer goes, just turn the oven off, open its door and leave the loaf there to wake up to. It's also great at teatime, or in a lunchbox.

SERVES 10–12

For the banana bread

100g (3½oz / ½ cup) virgin coconut oil,
  melted, plus more for the tin (pan)
100g (3½oz / ¾ cup) walnuts
100g (3½oz / 1 cup) ground almonds
pinch of sea salt flakes
generous pinch of ground nutmeg
1 tsp ground cinnamon
2 tsp baking powder
100g (3½oz / 1 cup) oat bran
100g (3½oz / ¾ cup) flaxseeds or
  golden linseeds
100g (3½oz / ⅓ cup) runny honey
2 tsp vanilla extract
500g (1lb 2oz) banana flesh (from
  4–5 bananas), as ripe as possible

Toppings I love:

peaches, raspberries, ricotta or
  mascarpone cheese and honey
  or honeycomb
figs, yogurt and honeycomb
butter and honey or honeycomb or jam,
  or date syrup or maple syrup
yogurt and honey or honeycomb and
  a sprinkle of toasted nuts, seeds or
  granola, with fresh fruit
yogurt and berries or fruit compote, with
  a sprinkle of granola
nut butter, jam or squashed berries
  or banana
home-made chocolate spread or ganache
  (see pages 82, 90 or 144)
ice cream and melted chocolate
tahini, maple syrup, chopped dates or
  figs and sesame seeds or walnuts

Preheat the oven to 180°C/350°F/gas mark 4. Oil a 18 x 11 x 8cm (7 x 4½ x 3in) loaf tin (pan) and line the base and sides with a piece of baking parchment, so it's easy to remove the bread after baking.

In a food processor, process the walnuts until fine. Add the ground almonds, salt, nutmeg, cinnamon, baking powder, oat bran and seeds and process to combine. Use a spatula to scrape the ingredients off the bottom of the bowl and process once more.

Add the coconut oil, honey, vanilla and bananas and process until as smooth as possible. (If there are a few lumps of banana, that's fine.)

Pour the batter into the prepared tin (pan) and bake for 40 minutes. Reduce the oven temperature to 160°C/325°F/gas mark 3, rotate the tin (pan) and bake for a further 30–40 minutes, until a skewer inserted in the centre comes out just clean and the top of the loaf is dark golden brown and firm to the touch. Leave to cool in the tin (pan), then remove from the tin (pan) and serve with any of the toppings listed on the left, or just with butter.

Keep in an airtight container in the fridge for at least 1 week, or cut and freeze in slices for up to 1 month (see page 17). When it's less fresh, it's nice warmed up a little in the oven, on a baking tray (sheet) lined with baking parchment.

Variation: Raisins or other dried fruit, whole nuts and other seeds are all nice additions to the batter, each lending a little more flavour and texture.

Chestnut flour drop scones with baked lemon thyme and honey peaches

Drop scones are little pancakes, almost the size of American versions but a little daintier. We used to cook them straight on the hot plate of our AGA, as in the photo opposite. They were always such a treat in the morning or at teatime for my brother, sister and me, served with my mother's home-made jam. Baked fresh seasonal fruit is also a lovely accompaniment. They are often made with plain (all-purpose) flour, but I use chestnut flour, as its nuttiness in the little light, plump pancakes is sublime with the succulent, sweet and fragrant peaches. As chestnut flour is slightly dense, I whisk egg whites to lighten the mix, but they can still be made in minutes, I promise. Whip them up for late-summer breakfasts and everyone will be happy.

MAKES 16, SERVES 3–5

For the peaches
6 ripe-but-still-firm peaches
50–70g (1¾–2½oz / ¼ cup) runny honey
6 sprigs of lemon thyme, plus more
  to serve (optional)
½ vanilla pod (bean), split lengthways,
  seeds scraped out

For the drop scones
150g (5½oz / 1 cup) chestnut flour
1 tsp baking powder
200g (7oz / generous ¾ cup) whole milk,
  or unsweetened nut or other
  plant-based milk
2 eggs, separated
1 tsp vanilla extract
pinch of sea salt flakes
unsalted butter or virgin coconut oil,
  to cook
ricotta, mascarpone cheese or natural
  yogurt, honey or honeycomb, to serve

Start by baking the peaches. Preheat the oven to 180°C/350°F/gas mark 4. Cut the peaches into quarters and remove the stones. Place the quarters on a baking tray (sheet), then drizzle over the honey – use the smaller or larger amount, according to your taste – and scatter with the sprigs of lemon thyme and vanilla seeds. Stir the mix around a bit to disperse the seeds, then add the empty pod (bean), too. Bake for 30 minutes, or until a skewer slides easily into the centre of a piece. Set aside.

In a bowl, whisk together the chestnut flour and baking powder. Pour in the milk, egg yolks and vanilla extract and whisk until smooth. Whisk the egg whites and salt in a separate bowl until light and fluffy, then fold them lightly into the batter until completely incorporated.

Heat a large frying pan (skillet) and add a film of butter or coconut oil. Using a small ladle, pour small pancakes about 7–8cm (3in) diameter on to the hot pan. Cook for 30 seconds–1 minute on each side, until golden brown, then remove to a plate lined with a couple of pieces of kitchen paper. If you can't serve them immediately, keep them warm in a low oven while you cook the remaining drop scones, using up the batter.

Serve the drop scones warm with the warm peaches, discarding the cooked lemon thyme sprigs and vanilla pod (bean). Add the ricotta, mascarpone or yogurt, honey or honeycomb and a sprinkling of fresh lemon thyme leaves, if you like. (Chestnut or lavender honey are especially lovely with these.)

Store any leftover peaches in a sealed container in the fridge for about 5 days and enjoy them with yogurt and granola, or on toast or banana bread with ricotta. The drop scones must be eaten fresh, so are one of the very few things I don't recommend storing.

Apple and almond baked porridge (oatmeal)

Baked porridge (oatmeal) is made a little like rice pudding, though the oats make it much more set. It's warming, lovely and yummy and I could very easily eat it every morning of winter, just as I could eat baked apples every evening for pudding. Stewed, made into sauces, used in crumbles or baked as they are here, there are so many wonderful ways that Bramley apples can warm us up during the colder months and when they are added to the rest of the ingredients in this recipe, this baked porridge (oatmeal) will certainly do that, keeping you going on a chilly morning. The slight tartness of the apples, the sweet dried fruit, the creamy, subtly spiced porridge (oatmeal) with its hint of cinnamon and nutmeg, the crunchy toasted almond top… it's a real treat for breakfast and very simple to make.

SERVES 2–3

For the baked apples

2 large Bramley (cooking) apples, about 450g (1lb) total weight

80g (2¾oz / ½ cup) mixed sultanas (golden raisins), raisins and currants

a few knobs of unsalted butter (optional)

For the porridge

70g (2½oz / ¾ cup) rolled oats

couple of pinches of ground cinnamon

generous grating of nutmeg

1 tbsp maple syrup

1 tsp vanilla extract

500g (1lb 2oz / 2 cups) unsweetened almond milk, or any other milk

50g (1¾oz / ⅔ cup) flaked (slivered) almonds

The night before, preheat the oven to 180°C/350°F/gas mark 4. Core the apples and fill the holes with the dried fruit, adding knobs of butter to top them off, if you like. (Any dried fruit that won't fit can be added to the oat mix the next day.) Put the stuffed apples into a 18 x 13 x 5cm (7 x 5 x 2in) or a similar sized ovenproof dish and bake for 15 minutes, or until just bursting. Leave the oven door ajar and let the apples stay there overnight. You can easily do this in the morning, if you've got the time.

In the morning, preheat the oven to 180°C/350°F/gas mark 4 once more. Mix the oats, spices, maple syrup, vanilla extract and milk in a bowl, then pour into the dish and around the apples. Sprinkle over the flaked (slivered) almonds and bake for 30 minutes, until the mix is bubbling and the top is golden brown.

Serve while it's hot, in warmed bowls. It's lovely with a little extra milk, natural yogurt, honey or maple syrup and a little more of the spices if you like; or with cream, brown sugar and a little Calvados or whisky on an especially cold and blustery morning… or indeed, any morning!

Variation: Cooked quince or pears would also work well and, as the seasons change, you can easily replace the apples with other fruits: think rhubarb baked with a little sugar and orange juice in early spring; or raspberries and apricots in the summer; or blueberries, blackberries and plums as autumn approaches. Bake stone fruits and harder fruits first, then add softer fruits such as berries to the oat and milk mix before returning to the oven for the final 30-minute bake.

Toasted pecan, banana and date muffins

I love these for breakfast, with natural yogurt, extra toasted pecans or a sprinkling of granola. They're also lovely with fresh fruit, or try them with Baked bananas with lime and coconut cream (see page 168) and serve them warm as a dessert. The wholegrain flour, earthy rapeseed (canola) oil and toasted nuts are all great together, while the puréed dates and mashed bananas keep the muffins so soft and moist, with just the right balance of sweetness. They're very quick and simple, too, with everything mixed in one saucepan.

MAKES 12

60g (2oz / ¼ cup) extra virgin cold-pressed rapeseed (canola) oil, plus more for the tin

200g (7oz / 1½ cups) pitted dates

200g (7oz / generous ¾ cup) boiling water

2 tsp bicarbonate of soda (baking soda)

200g (7oz) ripe banana flesh, plus more bananas, sliced, to top (3–4 in total)

100g (3½oz / generous ⅓ cup) unsweetened almond milk, or any other milk

2 tsp lemon juice

2 eggs, lightly beaten

130g (4¾oz / 1 cup) wholegrain wheat or spelt flour

60g (2oz / ½ cup) pecan nuts, toasted and roughly chopped (see page 102)

1 tsp ground cinnamon

1 tsp ground mixed spice

1½ tsp baking powder

Preheat the oven to 180°C/350°F/gas mark 4. Line a 12-hole muffin tin (pan) with paper cases, or squares of baking parchment. If using squares of baking parchment, lightly oil the tin first, so the parchment will stick to it.

Cover the dates with the boiling water in a saucepan over a medium-high heat, then return to the boil. Reduce the heat slightly, stirring occasionally, until the dates have absorbed all the water, then mash them with a spoon to form a paste. Remove from the heat. While still hot, mix in the bicarbonate of soda (baking soda), continuing to stir until the fizzing stops.

Mash in the bananas with a fork. Add the almond milk, lemon juice, rapeseed (canola) oil and eggs and mix everything together well.

Add all the remaining ingredients and stir lightly until completely combined. Divide the batter between the paper cases and top each muffin with a 1cm- (½in-) thick round of banana, pushing it into the mix slightly. Bake for 10 minutes, then rotate the tin (pan) and bake for a further 10 minutes, until golden brown, firm but bouncy to the touch, and a skewer inserted in the centre of a muffin comes out clean. Leave to cool and enjoy.

These will keep for up to 5 days in an airtight container in the fridge and they freeze well, too, for at least 1 month.

Variation 1: Try a granola version for a great extra crunch and added flavour: fold in 100–200g (3½–7oz / ¾–1⅔ cups) granola to the batter at the end, and sprinkle with another 100–200g (3½–7oz / ¾–1⅔ cups) before baking, depending on how crunchy you want them.

Variation 2: Make a quick sticky toffee-like date sauce for the muffins by soaking a large handful of soft dates in warm water to cover, then blending with a hand-held blender, adding a little coconut milk until you get the right consistency, then sea salt to taste.

Buckwheat, rum and raisin *Kaiserschmarrn* with plum compote and vanilla cream

An absolutely sumptuous breakfast, though probably a later one if you're going to be adding the rum! Fluffy layers of a soufflé-like pancake, speckled with rum-plumped raisins, oozing with the sweet juices of plums, with a cloud of whipped vanilla cream. *Kaiserschmarrn* are a type of Austrian shredded pancake, though I've deviated slightly from the authentic recipe here and used buckwheat instead of white wheat flour, which adds its distinct toasted flavour and is lovely with the raisins and rum.

MAKES 2 LARGE PANCAKES, SERVES 6–8

For the compote

6 large firm-ish red-purple plums, about 450g (1lb) total weight, each pitted and cut into 8 (or quartered, if small)
100g (3½oz / generous ⅓ cup) water
50g (1¾oz / ¼ cup) light brown muscovado or coconut sugar
½ tbsp vanilla extract

For the *kaisershmarrn*

85g (3oz / ½ cup) raisins
65g (2¼oz / ¼ cup) rum, plus more to serve (optional, see Variation, below)
250g (9oz / 1 cup) whole milk, or any other unsweetened plant-based milk
125g (4½oz / scant 1 cup) buckwheat flour
½ tsp baking powder
3 eggs, separated
1 tsp vanilla extract
25g (1oz) light brown muscovado or coconut sugar, plus more to serve
unsalted butter, to cook

For the vanilla cream

250g (9oz / 1 cup) double (heavy) cream
⅓ vanilla pod (bean), split lengthways, seeds scraped out

Place the plums in a saucepan with the water, sugar and vanilla extract and cook over a low heat until soft. Remove from the heat and set aside. In a bowl, cover the raisins with the rum and leave to soak.

Whip the cream with the vanilla seeds until it billows, but do not over-whip. Set aside somewhere cool.

Whisk the milk with the flour, baking powder, egg yolks and vanilla extract. Separately whisk the egg whites until soft peaks form, then gradually add the sugar, still whisking. Fold into the flour mix until just combined.

Melt a knob of butter in a frying pan (skillet) with a base about 20cm (8in) in diameter, making sure the surface is completely coated with butter, then pour half the mixture in like a pancake. Sprinkle over half the raisins and some splashes of rum and cook for about 3 minutes, until the edges look golden. Flip over and cook for another 2–3 minutes: the pancake should feel just firm. Flip back so the raisins are on top, then remove from the heat, roughly cut up, sprinkle with a little sugar and serve immediately, topping with half the plums and cream and some more splashes of rum.

Repeat the process to cook the second pancake.

This is best eaten fresh, though any leftover plums and cream will keep in the fridge for about 5 days.

Variation: If you'd prefer to leave out the rum, substitute it with black tea.

Fennel seed, orange and date granola,
or granola bars

I love a granola to be packed full of delicious textures and flavours like this version. Slightly harder rye flakes are combined with soft and creamy oats and crisp, nutty spelt flakes along with crunchy seeds and chewy dates. Honey, fennel seeds and a little orange and spice then oomph it all up to create something wonderful to eat every morning. It's more of a flaky than an extra-crunchy granola. If you need breakfast on the go, try the granola bars, too. The recipe is nearly-but-not-quite identical, so I give both below.

**MAKES 18–20 SERVINGS OF GRANOLA,
OR ABOUT 22 BARS**

For the granola
300g (10½oz / 3 cups) rolled oats
200g (7oz / 2½ cups) rye flakes
100g (3½oz / 1¼ cups) spelt flakes
100g (3½oz / ¾ cup) pumpkin seeds
100g (3½oz / ¾ cup) sunflower seeds
100g (3½oz / ¾ cup) sesame seeds
20g (¾oz / 4 tsp) fennel seeds
2 tsp ground mixed spice
generous pinch of sea salt flakes
finely grated zest of 2 oranges, plus
   120g (4¼oz / ½ cup) orange juice
150g (5½oz / ⅔ cup) extra virgin
   cold-pressed rapeseed (canola) oil
150g (5½oz / scant ½ cup) honey
150g (5½oz / generous 1 cup) pitted
   dates, roughly chopped

For the granola bars
150g (5½oz / ¾ cup) melted virgin
   coconut oil, plus more for the tin (pan)
150g (5½oz / 1½ cups) rolled oats
100g (3½oz / 1¼ cups) rye flakes
50g (1¾oz / scant ½ cup) spelt flakes
50g (1¾oz / ⅓ cup) pumpkin seeds
50g (1¾oz / ⅓ cup) sunflower seeds
50g (1¾oz / ⅓ cup) sesame seeds
10g (2 tsp) fennel seeds
1 tsp ground mixed spice
pinch of sea salt flakes
150g (5½oz / generous 1 cup) pitted
   dates, chopped
finely grated zest of 1 orange, plus
   60g (2oz / ¼ cup) orange juice
150g (5½oz / scant ½ cup) honey

To make the granola, preheat the oven to 160°C/325°F/gas mark 3. Line 2 large baking trays (sheets) with baking parchment.

Mix all the dry ingredients together in a large bowl, from the oats to the sea salt. Mix the orange zest and juice, rapeseed (canola) oil and honey in a separate bowl. (If your honey has solidified, heat it a little until runny.) Add the liquids to the dry ingredients and mix well until everything is combined. Divide between the 2 trays (sheets) and bake for 20 minutes, or until golden brown, turning the trays halfway through baking and mixing the granola up roughly so there are some large and some smaller pieces, making sure to move the outside parts to the middle so that everything bakes evenly. Leave to cool, then mix in the chopped dates.

Stored in airtight jars, it will keep for at least 1 month. I love to serve it with fresh seasonal fruit or a compote and thick yogurt. Add an extra drizzle of honey if you want.

For the granola bars, oil a 30 x 20 x 3cm (12 x 8 x 1¼in) deep baking tray (brownie pan or similar) with a little coconut oil and line it with baking parchment. Preheat the oven to 160°C/325°F/gas mark 3.

Mix all the dry ingredients together in a large bowl, from the oats to the sea salt. Add the dates. Add the orange zest and juice, the melted coconut oil and honey. Mix everything well, then transfer to the tin (pan), placing a piece of baking parchment on top and smoothing it over, pressing to compress the mix, then smoothing over once more with a cranked or step palette knife.

Bake for 50–55 minutes, rotating the tin (pan) halfway through baking. Leave to cool completely, then cut horizontally with a serrated knife into 2.5cm (1in) slices, then turn the slices around and cut in half again to get 10 x 2.5cm (4 x 1in) bars. They will crumble a bit when cutting, but that's normal. Store in an airtight container; these will keep for at least 1 week in the fridge, and they freeze well, too, for up to 1 month.

Variation: Try using different flakes such as buckwheat, millet, quinoa, brown rice, puffed rice or amaranth. Buckwheat groats have a great crunch.

Spinach soufflé omelette with chives and goat's cheese

Oven-baked soufflés can seem daunting, but making a soufflé omelette is wonderfully easy and every bit as good as the baked version. Strictly speaking, there is only grilling (broiling) involved rather than baking, but I feel the techniques of baking – such as folding and whisking – make it worthy of inclusion here as a baking recipe! A sumptuous breakfast indeed. Just double the quantities for two people and use a larger pan.

SERVES 1

sea salt flakes and freshly ground
   black pepper
100g (3½oz / 3 cups) spinach leaves
2 eggs, separated
1 tbsp finely chopped chives, plus more
   to serve
unsalted butter or extra virgin olive oil,
   to cook
60g (2oz) soft goat's cheese
finely grated Parmesan cheese, to serve

Bring a medium pan of water to the boil and add a few pinches of salt. Drop in the spinach leaves to wilt briefly, then remove from the heat and strain them into a colander under a running cold tap. Squeeze out all the excess water and roughly chop the spinach.

Preheat the grill (broiler).

Place the egg yolks in a bowl, mix in the cooled spinach and chives and season well with salt and pepper. Start to whisk the egg whites in a separate bowl. Place a small frying pan (skillet), about 20cm (8in) in diameter, over a low heat with a knob of butter or a little oil. When the whites are fluffy and stiff, fold them into the egg yolk mix. Increase the heat under the frying pan (skillet). Pour the mixture into the frying pan (skillet) and cook for 2–3 minutes, until the edges are becoming golden. Sprinkle over the goat's cheese and place under the hot grill (broiler) for a few minutes, until the cheese melts and looks a little golden.

Remove the pan from the grill (broiler) and slide a palette knife round the edge. Ease one half of the omelette over the other and tilt the whole lot out on to a warmed plate. Finish with grated Parmesan, chopped chives and black pepper and serve immediately.

Bacon-and-egg pies with spring onions (scallions) and tomato

I've played around a little with this recipe after tasting a delicious pie on a trip to New Zealand. That one was made with puff pastry, but I developed an einkorn pastry (pie crust) for these. Its slight graininess and rich taste work brilliantly with the salty bacon and creamy egg and crème fraîche mixture, the juicy tomatoes and the kick of the spring onions (scallions). Einkorn is one of the earliest cultivated varieties of wheat. It only has single grains on either side of the ear, hence its name einkorn, meaning 'one corn'.

A great start to the day, at home or on the go. On a relaxed morning, these are good for taking a little time over. Otherwise, bake the shells the night before, then fill and bake again in the morning. You can freeze the raw pastry (pie dough), as shells or just wrapped in cling film (plastic wrap), for at least 1 month.

MAKES 6 INDIVIDUAL 10 X 3CM (4 X 1¼IN) TARTS

For the pastry (pie dough)
115g (4oz / ½ cup / 1 stick) cold unsalted butter, cut into cubes, plus more for the tins (pans)
225g (8oz / 1⅔ cups) wholegrain einkorn flour, plus more to dust
1 tsp sea salt flakes
1 egg, lightly beaten, plus 1 egg yolk to glaze

For the filling
12 rashers (slices) of streaky bacon, roughly chopped
5 eggs, lightly beaten
120g (4¼oz / ½ cup) crème fraîche
50g (1¾oz) spring onions (scallions), finely chopped, plus more to serve
1 tomato, about 80g (2¾oz), finely chopped
sea salt flakes and freshly ground black pepper

Butter six 10 x 3cm (4 x 1¼in) tart tins (pans), preferably with loose bottoms. In a freestanding mixer fitted with a paddle, or using your fingertips, mix the flour, salt and butter until it resembles crumbs. Add the egg and mix until it just comes together. If the dough is sticky and warm, wrap it in cling film (plastic wrap) and chill for 30 minutes. If it is cool, just continue.

Weigh the pastry (pie dough) and then divide it equally into 6. Between 2 pieces of lightly floured baking parchment, roll each piece into a circle about 3mm (⅛in) thick. Line each tart shell with 1 circle of pastry, pushing the dough into the corners of the tins (pans) to get rid of any air bubbles, pressing it round the edges and folding over any excess. Trim the edges with a knife. Chill in the fridge for 30 minutes–1 hour.

Meanwhile, fry the bacon in a dry pan until the fat has melted away and the bacon is crisp in places. Remove from the pan and place on kitchen paper to blot off excess fat.

Preheat the oven to 180°C/350°F/gas mark 4. Make the pie filling by mixing together all the ingredients, then season with salt and pepper.

Line each pastry shell with baking parchment and fill with baking beans. Blind bake the pastry shells for 10 minutes. Remove the baking beans and bake for a further 10 minutes until golden brown. Leave to cool slightly, then carefully brush each pastry shell with egg yolk and bake for 1–2 further minutes, or until the yolk has dried.

Fill each shell with the egg mix, place in the oven, then reduce the oven temperature to 160°C/325°F/gas mark 3. Bake for 15–20 minutes, or until set. Leave to cool slightly, then carefully remove from the tins (pans).

Serve warm or cold with a salad, if you like, and extra chopped spring onions (scallions). Keep any leftovers in the fridge for up to 4 days.

Green pea, broad bean (fava bean) and feta cakes with mint

I really enjoy having friends over for relaxed and abundant breakfasts, especially in the summer when all the gorgeous vegetables come along. These cakes are light and full of fresh flavours from the green beans and peas to mint, lemon and salty feta. Top them with whatever you like; I've given my favourite options here.

MAKES 3

For the cakes
sea salt flakes and freshly ground
   black pepper
200g (7oz / ⅔ cup) broad beans (fava
   beans), fresh or frozen
150g (5½oz / 1 cup) green peas, fresh
   or frozen
1 tbsp extra virgin olive oil
1 egg, lightly beaten
10g (¼oz) mint leaves, finely chopped,
   plus more to serve (optional)
finely grated zest of ½–1 unwaxed
   lemon, to taste, plus more to serve
   (optional)
60g (2oz) feta cheese, plus more
   to serve (optional)

To serve (all optional)
poached or hard-boiled eggs
toasted pumpkin seeds
chilli oil
avocado
natural yogurt
chive or other herb flowers

Preheat the oven to 200°C/400°F/gas mark 6. Line a small baking tray (sheet) with baking parchment.

Bring 2 small saucepans of water to the boil and add a pinch of salt to each. Drop the beans into one pan and the peas into the other and boil for a few minutes. Strain the peas through a colander. Strain the beans through a colander, allow them to cool a little, then squeeze the soft, bright green inner beans out of their shells. (Discard the bean shells.)

Put the shelled beans and peas in a food processor with the olive oil, egg, mint, salt, pepper and lemon zest to taste. Process a little until the mix comes together, but there is still some texture. Taste for seasoning.

Crumble in the feta and mix in lightly. Divide the mix into 3 and pat into circles on the prepared tray (sheet), each about 10cm (4in) wide and a bit less than 2cm (¾in) deep. Bake for 15 minutes, or until they feel firm.

Lift them off the tray (sheet) with a spatula and serve immediately, with any or all of the serving suggestions: a poached or hard-boiled egg, mint leaves, toasted pumpkin seeds, chilli oil, avocado, feta, salt and pepper, lemon zest, natural yogurt and chive or other herb flowers.

Breakfast Gruyère gougères with crispy bacon and watercress

Gougères are like savoury profiteroles with lots of cheese… sound pretty good? Hot from the oven, these light and puffy cheesy balls are filled with crispy bacon and fresh and peppery watercress. I love serving them as part of a delicious breakfast spread, or they make great canapés, too. The mature (sharp) and earthy flavour of the Gruyère is lifted by the addition of wholegrain flour in the pastry.

Makes 16

125g (4½oz / ½ cup) whole milk
1 tsp sea salt flakes
115g (4oz / ½ cup / 1 stick) unsalted butter
125g (4½oz / ½ cup) water
90g (3¼oz / ⅔ cup) strong white wheat flour
90g (3¼oz / ⅔ cup) strong wholegrain wheat flour
3 eggs, about 160g (5¾oz) cracked total weight, lightly beaten
70g (2½oz) Gruyère cheese, grated
freshly ground black pepper
cayenne pepper
streaky bacon, cream cheese, chives and watercress or rocket (arugula), to serve

Preheat the oven to 200°C/400°F/gas mark 6. Line a baking tray (sheet) with baking parchment. Fit a piping (pastry) bag with a 1.5cm (⅝in) nozzle (tip).

Warm the milk, salt and butter in a saucepan with the water until the butter has melted. Add both flours and mix to a paste which is just catching on the bottom of the pan. It should stick together in a rough ball. Remove from the heat. Using a wooden spoon, gradually add the eggs (reserve 25g / 1oz of them for glazing), beating until smooth, shiny and – when you lift some of it up on the spoon – the choux pastry just holds and keeps its shape.

Mix in 30g (1oz / ¼ cup) of the cheese, some twists of black pepper and a pinch of cayenne pepper. Fill the piping (pastry) bag and pipe out 16 mounds, each about 5cm (2in) in diameter. Brush the top of each mound with the reserved egg. Sprinkle over the remaining Gruyère, pressing it on lightly so it sticks, and bake for 15 minutes, until golden brown.

Open the oven door, reduce the oven temperature to 100°C/225°F/gas mark ¼, then close the door and cook the gougères for a final 10 minutes to dry them out. The centres can be a bit soft, but you are looking for crisp rolls.

Fry the bacon until crispy; I cook about 2 rashers (slices) for each gougère. Cut the gougères horizontally, fill with a little cream cheese and chives, add the bacon, then the watercress or rocket (arugula). These are best eaten fresh.

After piping the raw gougères, they can be frozen on the tray (sheet). Once frozen, lift them off the paper and store in a container. Bake from frozen, sprinkling over the cheese and adding a few more minutes to the baking time. Store in the freezer for at least 1 month.

Keep leftover gougères in an airtight container for up to 5 days, warming them up before serving. They're great filled or topped with other breakfast foods, such as eggs, smoked salmon and ham, or hummus, tomatoes and mild creamy goat's cheese, or indeed yummy just by themselves.

Caramelized red onion, parsley and Cheddar scones

Waking up to these freshly baked, soft and light cheese scones in the morning is a real joy. The sweet, caramelized red onion, rich and nutty wholegrain flour, strong Cheddar and hint of mustard is all just scrumptious. Eat them as they are, or cut them in half and spread with butter. When they're less fresh, toast them and top with smoked salmon, scrambled eggs and chopped chives as an exceptionally delicious start to the day, though they're great with fillings in packed lunches, too.

MAKES 12

1 red onion, about 170g (6oz) trimmed weight
1 tbsp extra virgin cold-pressed rapeseed (canola) oil, or extra virgin olive oil
sea salt flakes
1 tbsp balsamic or red wine vinegar
1 tbsp light brown muscovado or coconut sugar
freshly ground black pepper
250g (9oz / scant 1 cup) wholegrain spelt flour, plus more to dust
3 tsp baking powder
90g (3¼oz) mature (sharp) Cheddar cheese, grated
60g (2oz / ¼ cup / ½ stick) unsalted butter, cold and cut into cubes
2 tsp English mustard, plus ½ tsp for the top
80g (2¾oz / ⅓ cup) buttermilk or natural yogurt, plus 20g (¾oz / 4 tsp) for the top
1 egg, plus 1 egg yolk
20g (¾oz) flat-leaf parsley leaves, finely chopped

Halve the red onion, then finely slice in semi-circles. Heat the oil in a frying pan (skillet) and add the onion with ½ tsp salt. Reduce the heat and cook until golden brown. Add the vinegar, sugar and a bit more salt and pepper to taste. Cook for a little longer, until caramelized, golden and soft. Leave to cool.

Preheat the oven to 200°C/400°F/gas mark 6 and line a baking tray (sheet) with baking parchment.

Combine the flour, baking powder, ½ tsp more salt and 60g (2oz / ⅔ cup) of the Cheddar in a bowl or freestanding mixer fitted with a paddle. Add the butter and combine until the mix resembles crumbs. Now, in a separate bowl, mix the 2 tsp mustard, the buttermilk, the 1 egg and a pinch of black pepper and add to the flour mix. Roughly chop the onions and add them to the dough along with the parsley, then mix until just incorporated.

On a floured surface, flatten the dough into a square about 2cm (¾in) high and 16cm (6¼in) along each side. Cut it down the middle, turn the 2 rectangles of dough around, then cut each into 3. Now cut each section of dough into 2 triangles, you want 12 in total. Transfer to the prepared tray (sheet).

Mix together the egg yolk with the remaining ½ tsp mustard, the 20g (¾oz / 4 tsp) buttermilk or yogurt and the remaining 30g (1oz / ⅓ cup) cheese. Divide the cheese and yolk mix between the scone triangles, using your hands or a pastry brush to spread it evenly over the top of each.

Bake for 10 minutes, or until golden brown on the top and bottom. Serve warm from the oven.

Store any remaining scones in an airtight container for 5 days, or freeze for at least 1 month.

Variation: Try adding cooked bacon lardons to the scone dough before baking.

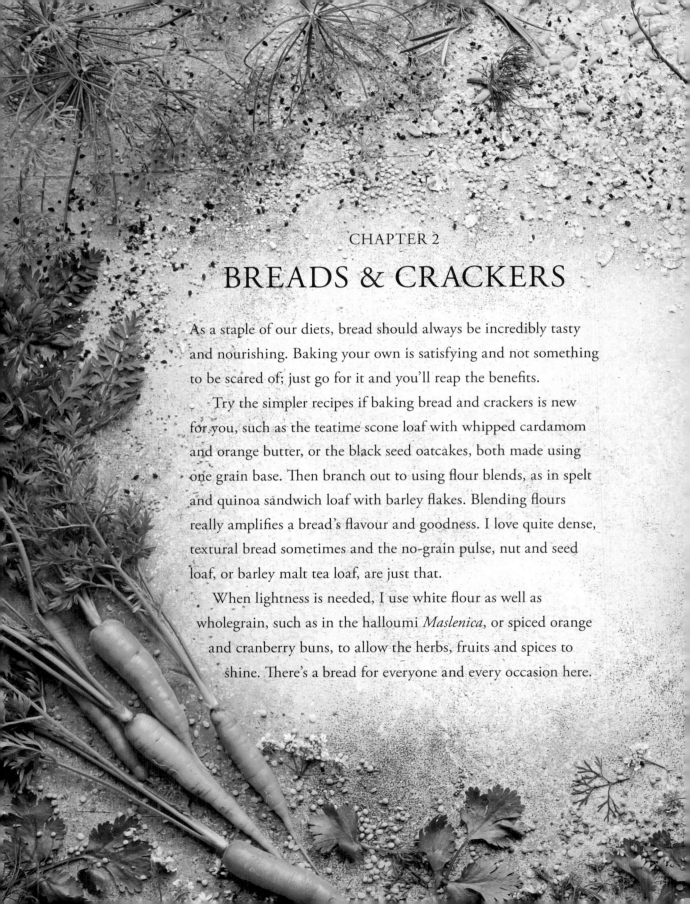

CHAPTER 2

BREADS & CRACKERS

As a staple of our diets, bread should always be incredibly tasty and nourishing. Baking your own is satisfying and not something to be scared of; just go for it and you'll reap the benefits.

Try the simpler recipes if baking bread and crackers is new for you, such as the teatime scone loaf with whipped cardamom and orange butter, or the black seed oatcakes, both made using one grain base. Then branch out to using flour blends, as in spelt and quinoa sandwich loaf with barley flakes. Blending flours really amplifies a bread's flavour and goodness. I love quite dense, textural bread sometimes and the no-grain pulse, nut and seed loaf, or barley malt tea loaf, are just that.

When lightness is needed, I use white flour as well as wholegrain, such as in the halloumi *Maslenica*, or spiced orange and cranberry buns, to allow the herbs, fruits and spices to shine. There's a bread for everyone and every occasion here.

Suffolk spelt, quinoa and barley loaf

This loaf is an ode to where I grew up, where the grains and oilseed rape are all grown locally. The earthy rapeseed (canola) oil, the nutty barley and spelt and the grassy quinoa combine to create the deepest and most delicious, almost hoppy flavour, enhanced by the overnight rise. It's got a lovely, slightly dense crumb and a great bite from the quinoa grains, along with its gorgeous crust, a very important factor for me when it comes to a good loaf of bread! It's simple to make and great for breakfast, sandwiches, with soup… a really reliable, quick and easy, nutritious loaf.

MAKES 1

75g (2½oz / ½ cup) quinoa
500g (1lb 2oz / generous 4 cups) wholegrain spelt flour, plus more to dust
75g (2½oz / generous ¾ cup) barley flakes, or other flakes such as oats or millet
3½ tsp sea salt flakes
½ tbsp dried yeast
250g (9oz / 1 cup) lukewarm water
50g (1¾oz / ¼ cup) extra virgin cold-pressed rapeseed (canola) oil, plus more to handle the dough
50g (1¾oz / scant ¼ cup) natural yogurt
1 tsp honey

Put the quinoa in a saucepan with 200g (7oz / generous ¾ cup) water. Bring to the boil, then reduce the heat to a simmer and cook for about 10 minutes, or until the water has been absorbed and the quinoa is cooked, but still a little al dente and sticking slightly to the pan. Turn off the heat and set aside to cool.

In a large bowl, mix the flour, cooked and cooled quinoa, barley flakes and salt. Make a well in the centre, add the yeast, and then pour the warm water on to dissolve it. Add the oil, yogurt and honey, then mix with a wooden spoon until the ingredients come together.

Either place the dough in a freestanding mixer fitted with a dough hook and knead for 10 minutes, or turn it out on to a floured work surface and knead by hand. If the dough feels sticky, add a little flour to your hands, the top of the dough and the work surface to help the kneading. When the dough feels smooth and strong, place it in an oiled bowl, dabbing the top of the dough with a little oil, too. It's fine if it still feels a bit sticky. Leave the dough in a cool-ish place, cover with a tea towel and let it rise overnight or for 8 hours. If you are leaving it for longer than 8 hours, prove it in the fridge, then let it come to room temperature before continuing with the next steps.

Line a baking tray (sheet) with baking parchment. Turn the risen dough out on to a work surface, and work it to punch out the air, then knead for 1 minute. Shape the dough into a round, place it on the prepared tray (sheet) and let it rise for another 1 hour, or until just about doubled in size. When risen, slice 3 slits over the top of the loaf with a sharp knife.

Preheat the oven to 220°C/425°C/gas mark 7. Place the loaf on its baking tray (sheet) into the oven. I sometimes throw a small glass of water into the bottom of the oven, too, to create steam and give the loaf more of a crust. Bake for 10 minutes. Reduce the oven temperature to 190°C/375°C/gas mark 5 and bake for a further 25–30 minutes, until a good, golden-brown crust has formed and the bottom of the loaf sounds hollow when tapped. Let it cool on the tray (sheet).

This keeps for at least 5 days in a cool place and freezes well, too, either as a whole loaf or in slices (see page 17).

Variations: After the 8-hour rise, divide the dough into 3, knock out the air and roll each third into a ball. Make either crackers or pizzas, as below, or a mixture. On a floured surface, thinly roll each round into a roughly 30cm (12in) diameter circle. Bake all at 200°C/400°F/gas mark 6.

Multi-seed crackers

Place the round of dough on a floured baking tray about 32 x 23cm (13 x 9in), and gently push it out to the edges, making it as thin as possible. Brush with water and sprinkle over a mixture of seeds, up to 120g (4¼oz / scant 1 cup); I use pumpkin, sunflower and sesame. Press them in lightly, sprinkle with sea salt flakes and bake for 30 minutes, turning the tray halfway, until crisp. If it is crunchy around the edges but still soft in the middle, break it up and rearrange so the soft parts are on the edges of the tray, reduce the oven temperature to 120°C/250°F/gas mark ½ and leave for 30 minutes–1 hour to dry out. These also work without seeds, or you can add oats, extra barley flakes or other flakes, or spices such as fennel and mustard seeds.

Pizza bianca with potatoes, rosemary and sea salt

Place the round of dough on a floured baking tray (sheet), pushing it to the edges so it's as thin as possible. Drizzle with extra virgin olive oil. Arrange over 300g (10½oz) finely sliced cooked potatoes, break over a few sprigs of rosemary and leave to rise for 1 more hour. Drizzle with extra virgin olive oil, sprinkle with sea salt and bake for 20 minutes, or until the base is dry to the touch and golden brown.

Rye, beetroot (beet), walnut, sultana (golden raisin) and caraway loaf

This loaf is just bursting with nourishing ingredients, flavours and textures, from the complex notes of the slightly sour rye and treacly molasses to the earthy beetroot (beet), and from the crunch of the walnuts and aromatic caraway to the sweet, plump sultanas (golden raisins). As you bite into a slice, with its gorgeous crisp crust and moist-dense centre, you'll already be cutting the next! As rye contains less gluten than wheat and spelt, it creates a heavier and slightly more dense bread… which is a good thing, in the case of this loaf.

I love the taste of caraway seeds, but leave them out if you prefer.

MAKES 1

1 tbsp extra virgin cold-pressed
  rapeseed (canola) oil
375g (13oz / 1½ cups) lukewarm water
30g (1oz) molasses
2 tsp dried yeast
225g (8oz / 1½ cups) rye flour
225g (8oz / 1½ cups) dark rye flour
2 tsp sea salt flakes
60g (2oz / ⅓ cup) sultanas
  (golden raisins)
60g (2oz / ½ cup) walnuts,
  roughly chopped
1½ tsp caraway seeds (optional)
150g (5½oz / 1 cup) grated beetroot
  (about 1 beetroot / beet)

Oil the base and sides of a 900g (2lb) loaf tin (pan) with the oil; mine is 21 x 11 x 7cm (8¼ x 4¼ x 2¾in). Line the base with baking parchment.

In a small bowl or measuring jug, combine the warm water, molasses and yeast well. Leave for 10 minutes; the mixture will form a frothy top.

Combine the flours and salt in a bowl, then incorporate the sultanas (golden raisins), walnuts and caraway seeds. Add the grated beetroot (beet) to the yeast mix, stir it in, then add this to the dry ingredients, mixing with a wooden spoon. The dough should be quite sticky, but not runny. Place the dough in the prepared tin (pan), smooth out the top with a step or cranked palette knife or the back of a spoon, making sure there are no air gaps, especially in the corners of the tin (pan). Bang the tin (pan) once on a work surface, cover with a tea towel and leave to rise in a warm-ish place for 1 hour; the loaf should just be rising up over the edge of the tin (pan).

Preheat the oven to 200°C/400°F/gas mark 6. Bake for 20 minutes. Reduce the oven temperature to 190°C/375°F/gas mark 5 and bake for a further 30 minutes. Remove the loaf from the oven, carefully slide a knife around the edge, then remove it from the tin (pan). Reduce the oven temperature again, this time to 160°C/325°F/gas mark 3, place the loaf on a baking tray (sheet) and bake for a further 30 minutes.

Leave to cool for about 30 minutes on a wire rack, then serve. Store in a paper bag in the fridge (as it's quite a moist bread) for up to 5 days. This loaf freezes well, too, either whole or cut into slices (see page 17), for up to 1 month.

Yellow pea flour, quinoa, nut and seed loaf

Close to where I grew up in Suffolk, there are inspiring producers creating the most flavoursome and exciting foods. Not only are wheat, spelt and rye being milled and kombucha being brewed, but also quinoa, barley and pulses are being grown by an incredible company called Hodmedod's. It seemed only fitting to use some of their yellow pea flour and quinoa flakes in this loaf. Combined, they create a soft bread with a gorgeous distinct, savoury and earthy flavour, lifted up with that all-important salt and a little honey, all interspersed with crunchy nuts and seeds with their diverse tastes and textures. I love dense loaves like this with a simple salad at lunch. The bread is also great thinly sliced, toasted and served with cheese, dipped into hummus and guacamole, or used as a base for canapés.

Chickpea (garbanzo bean) flour also works in place of the yellow pea flour, while psyllium husk powder can be found in most health food shops and online.

MAKES 1

a little extra virgin cold-pressed rapeseed (canola) oil
100g (3½oz / scant 1 cup) yellow split pea flour (or see recipe introduction)
100g (3½oz / generous 1 cup) quinoa flakes
1 tbsp psyllium husk powder
2 tsp sea salt flakes
2 tbsp chia seeds
70g (2½oz / ½ cup) sunflower seeds
70g (2½oz / ½ cup) pumpkin seeds
70g (2½oz / generous ½ cup) walnut pieces or whole walnuts, roughly crumbled
70g (2½oz / ½ cup) whole almonds
70g (2½oz / ½ cup) whole pistachio nuts
200g (7oz / generous ¾ cup) cool water
1 tbsp runny honey

Preheat the oven to 180°C/350°F/gas mark 4. Oil the base and sides of an 18 x 11 x 8cm (7 x 4½ x 3in) loaf tin (pan) with the rapeseed (canola) oil. Line the base with baking parchment.

In a bowl, combine the flour, flakes, psyllium husk, salt and all the seeds and nuts and mix well. Add the water and honey and mix until well combined.

Spoon the mix into the prepared tin (pan). Dip your fingers in cool water and smooth over the top, pressing the bread mix well into the tin (pan) to ensure no air gaps, especially in the corners. With a flexible spatula or cranked or step palette knife, smooth out the top.

Bake for 25 minutes, then reduce the oven temperature to 160°C/325°F/gas mark 3 and bake for a further 20 minutes. The top should be a dark golden brown and firm to touch and the sides will just be coming away from the edges of the tin (pan). Leave to cool in the tin (pan) for 20 minutes, then tip it out to cool completely on a wire rack. Serve slices fresh or toasted and store the loaf (in the fridge, as it's quite a moist bread) for about 1 week.

You can freeze the loaf whole, or in slices (see page 17).

Halloumi, dill and soured cream *Maslenica*

Baked in a skillet or heavy-based pan or casserole dish, this is a traditional Bosnian loaf that I learned to bake from my dear friend, Olga. A very light, almost brioche-like dough is left to rise, then patted out lightly, spread with a mix of soured cream and melted butter and folded, creating lovely soft, buttery layers. Olga told me that often her family would wrap a coin or messages in foil and place them between the layers. I love the nutty taste of wholegrain flour, so I've added it here for more depth of flavour. Inspired by a gorgeous dill and halloumi loaf at the Greek café around the corner from where I live in London, I decided to add some dill and sliced halloumi to the layers. Eaten warm from the oven, the cheese oozing, or toasted over the next few days, it's simple and very tasty!

MAKES 1 LARGE LOAF

2 tsp dried yeast
1 tsp honey
200g (7oz / generous ¾ cup) lukewarm water
300g (10½oz / generous 2 cups) strong white wheat flour, plus 1 tsp, plus more to dust
200g (7oz / 1½ cups) strong wholegrain wheat flour
1 tsp sea salt flakes
2 eggs, lightly beaten
1 tbsp extra virgin olive oil, plus more for the pan, dish or skillet
20g (¾oz) dill, finely chopped
15g (½oz / 1 tbsp) unsalted butter
100g (3½oz / scant ½ cup) soured cream
freshly ground black pepper
250g (9oz) halloumi cheese, sliced a bit less than 5mm (¼in) thick

Mix together the yeast, honey and warm water and set aside for 15 minutes until a little foamy on top.

In a bowl, combine the flours and salt and make a well in the centre. Add the yeast mix, eggs, oil and half the dill, and bring the mix together with your hands, making sure all the ingredients are well combined.

Knead the mix for about 5 minutes on a lightly floured surface and then return to the bowl, cover with a towel and leave to prove for 1 hour, or until doubled in size.

Place the dough on a floured surface. Melt the butter and fetch a pastry brush. Mix together the soured cream and remaining dill with a few pinches of black pepper. Stretch and pat the dough into an oval measuring about 35cm (14in) long, 21cm (8½in) wide and a bit more than 1cm (½in) thick, using a rolling pin if necessary. Spread the right hand side of it with one-third of the butter, leaving 1cm (½in) of the edge uncovered, then top this buttered section with one-third of the soured cream, then one-third of the halloumi, again leaving the 1cm (½in) border. Fold over the left side without the topping, and press it around the edges to seal the filling in. Turn it over, then give it a quarter turn anti-clockwise, flattening out the dough. Use a rolling pin to form a rough oval again, rolling away from your body and making sure there is still enough flour on the work surface, and repeat the process twice more. After the third time, do not flatten it out, but instead shape the dough into a round. Oil a heavy-based ovenproof saucepan, casserole dish or skillet (mine has a 20cm / 8in base and is deep), put the loaf in with the seal at the bottom and leave to prove for another hour.

Preheat the oven to 200°C/400°F/gas mark 6. Bake the loaf for 20–25 minutes until golden brown; when the bottom is tapped, the loaf should sound hollow. It is normal for this loaf to drop slightly in the middle, due to the moisture of the filling. Eat warm from the oven while the cheese is melty. It's great with chutney.

Variation: Feta cheese works well between the layers, too.

Feta, olive and rosemary soda bread rolls

I first tasted proper soda bread on a memorable trip to Ballymaloe Cookery School in Ireland and it has since remained one of my favourite things to bake and eat. It's so fast and simple to make and the variations of fillings, flours and shapes are endless. Here I've gone for a deliciously nutritious blend of einkorn, spelt and rye flours, made into lovely soft rolls speckled with salty feta cheese, olives and aromatic rosemary.

Einkorn flour can be found in some health food shops, larger supermarkets and online. If you cannot find it, substitute the same amount of wholegrain spelt flour. Einkorn – along with emmer and spelt – has a higher protein content and a more fragile gluten structure than common wheat, therefore some people find these varieties of ancient grains easier to digest. I also love the rich flavours they add to my recipes.

MAKES 14

280g (10oz / 2 cups) wholegrain einkorn flour, plus more to dust
100g (3½oz / ¾ cup) wholegrain spelt flour
100g (3½oz / ¾ cup) rye flour
80g (2¾oz / scant 1 cup) rolled oats or other flakes, such as buckwheat or barley, plus more to sprinkle
2 tsp bicarbonate of soda (baking soda)
2 tsp sea salt flakes
10g (¼oz) finely chopped rosemary needles
140g (5oz) feta cheese, crumbled
400g (14oz / 1¾ cups) buttermilk
100g (3½oz / 1 cup) pitted black olives, roughly chopped

Preheat the oven to 190°C/375°F/gas mark 5 and line a baking tray (sheet) with baking parchment.

Mix together all the dry ingredients from the flours to the chopped rosemary in a bowl. Sprinkle over the feta. Make a well in the centre and mix in the buttermilk and black olives until just combined.

Turn the dough out on to a floured surface and divide it into 14 rolls, each 80g–90g (2¾–3¼oz). Place on the prepared baking tray (sheet), brush each roll with a little water and sprinkle with some extra oats.

Bake for 10 minutes, then rotate the tray (sheet), reduce the oven temperature to 180°C/350°F/gas mark 4 and bake for a further 10 minutes, until they are a good golden brown all over. When the bottom of a roll is tapped, it should sound hollow.

Eat as soon as possible, or keep any leftovers for about 5 days in an airtight container in a cool place. These also freeze well for up to 1 month.

Variation: The same amount of thyme would be lovely here, too, instead of rosemary, or mixed fresh herbs such as basil, parsley, thyme, rosemary... Or try adding a good handful of roughly chopped sun-dried tomatoes.

Black seed oatcakes

It is said that black seeds are the remedy for everything but death, and this scrumptiously different oatcake will certainly lift your spirits. The three kinds of black seeds all add a little bit of their distinct flavour and crunch to the crumbly, golden brown oat biscuit. Nigella seeds, with their pungent black pepper and onion notes, are a particularly good addition. These are great as a snack, in packed lunches, alongside a big salad for lunch, or with cheese, apples and chutney.

MAKES ABOUT 16

35g (1¼oz / heaping 2 tbsp) extra virgin cold-pressed rapeseed (canola) oil, plus more for the tin (pan)
100g (3½oz / generous 1 cup) rolled oats
40g (1½oz / ½ cup) oat bran
15g (½oz / 1 tbsp) poppy seeds
10g (¼oz / 2 tsp) black sesame seeds
1 tsp nigella seeds (optional)
½ tsp sea salt flakes
6 tbsp cold water, plus more to shape

Preheat the oven to 180°C/350°F/gas mark 4. Oil a 23cm (9in) loose-bottomed cake tin (pan) and line the base with baking parchment, using enough to come a bit up the sides of the tin (pan).

In a food processor, mix all the dry ingredients together, from the oats to the salt, to grind down the oats a little. Add the oil and water and mix again until everything comes together. Scrape the mix down from the edges of the bowl and mix for a final time.

Place the mixture into the prepared tin (pan) and spread it out to form a large cracker-like cake, flattening it down with your hands and then the back of a large spoon or a cranked or step palette knife. If you need to, add a few extra splashes of cold water to help the cracker stick together more and crumble less. Cut into 16 triangles using a small knife, cutting barely to the bottom of the tin (pan), so that when the oatcake is baked, the individual pieces will snap apart.

Bake for 35–37 minutes, or until golden brown. Leave to cool for about 10 minutes, then remove from the tin (pan), break up roughly along the scored knife marks and share. These will keep in an airtight container for at least 1 week.

Carrot and coriander crackers with mustard and anise seeds

Crunchy and with a subtle aroma of sweet spice from the anise, coriander and mustard seeds, these are such easy crackers and so versatile. Play around with the vegetables, using up old, floppy roots or courgettes (zucchini) hiding in the bottom drawer of your fridge, and try other herbs and spices; you could even make them into a flour-free open tart case, and top with your favourite things. The hemp seeds have a very subtle cheesy flavour, which make the crackers very moreish indeed, while ground almonds create that all-important crunch. Eat them alongside salads, dips and cheese, or just munch on them when you're peckish.

Hulled hemp seeds can be found in most health food shops and online. If you cannot find them, replace them with flaxseeds (golden linseeds).

MAKES 30

100g (3½oz) carrots, grated on the fine side of a box grater
120g (4¼oz / 1¼ cups) ground almonds
100g (3½oz / ¾ cup) hulled hemp seeds
2 tbsp dried coriander leaves
1 tsp anise seeds
1 tsp yellow mustard seeds
1 tsp coriander seeds
1 tsp sea salt flakes
a few pinches of freshly ground black pepper

Preheat the oven to 180°C/350°F/gas mark 4.

In a bowl, mix together the carrots, ground almonds, hemp seeds and dried coriander leaves. In a mortar and pestle, bash the anise, mustard and coriander seeds until just powdered (a few larger pieces of seed is fine). Add to the carrot mix with the salt and pepper.

Mix everything together with your hands and then form the mix into a flattish rectangle on a piece of baking parchment. Place another piece of baking parchment on top and roll the dough out into a rough rectangle about 36 x 21cm (14½ x 8½in) and no thicker than 3mm (⅛in), making sure that the centre is as thin as the edges.

Score roughly into strips about 9cm (3½in) long and 3cm (1¼in) wide. Place on a baking tray (sheet) and bake for 10 minutes. Remove from the oven and cut off the outer edges if they're getting crunchier, removing them from the tray. Cut the rest of the strips properly, separating the crackers from each other. Return to the oven for a further 8–10 minutes, keeping an eye on them so that they do not get too dark and removing any darker pieces from the edge of the tray when necessary; the crackers should be a golden brown and some will be just darkening a little on the edges. Leave to cool for 10 minutes on the tray, then enjoy.

Keep stored in an airtight container in a dry place for at least 1 week.

Variation: You can use fresh herbs in these crackers, too. Try up to 4 tbsp finely chopped coriander or flat-leaf parsley leaves, or a mixture with thyme leaves.

Teatime scone loaf with whipped cardamom and orange butter

Somewhere between a soda bread and scones, this is a wonderful rip-apart loaf. Buttermilk keeps it light and soft, though you can substitute yogurt, the dates add a subtle rich sweetness, while spelt and oats give nutty notes. You can whip it up quickly if friends come over at the last minute, and serve with mugs of tea and the delicately spiced, honeyed butter. Jam is great with it, too. Here I've used apricot and amaretto jam from Newton & Pott, an inspirational small-batch hand-made preserves company in Hackney, London. Any leftover butter is delicious on toast with jam, or with Spiced orange, apricot and cranberry buns (see page 66).

SERVES 6

For the bread

125g (4½oz / scant 1 cup) pitted dates, roughly chopped

100g (3½oz / generous ⅓ cup) hot black or rooibos tea or hot water

125g (4½oz / scant 1 cup) wholegrain spelt flour

2 tsp baking powder

¼ tsp ground allspice

¼ tsp sea salt flakes, plus a little for the glaze

30g (1oz / 2 tbsp) cold unsalted butter, cubed

1 heaped tsp molasses, just under 10g (¼oz)

75g (2¾oz / ⅓ cup) buttermilk or natural yogurt

1 egg

1 tbsp milk (any kind)

2 tbsp rolled or jumbo oats

For the butter

125g (4½oz / ½ cup / 1⅛ sticks) unsalted butter, at room temperature

pinch of sea salt flakes

finely grated zest of ½ orange, plus 1½ tbsp orange juice

1½ tsp ground cardamom

3 tsp honey

Preheat the oven to 200°C/400°F/gas mark 6. Line a baking tray (sheet) with baking parchment. Soak the dates in the tea or water for about 10 minutes.

Mix together the flour, baking powder, allspice and salt. Using a freestanding mixer fitted with a paddle, or by hand with your fingertips, work in the butter until the mix looks like crumbs. Drain the dates, then add them to the mix (don't worry if you add a little of their soaking juices), with the molasses and buttermilk, mixing lightly to form a soft, not too sticky dough.

Shape into a rough round on the prepared tray (sheet) and cut into 6 portions, stopping before reaching the tray (do not cut until the knife hits the tray). Beat the egg with a pinch of salt and the milk and brush on with a pastry brush. Sprinkle with the oats, patting them in lightly to stick.

Bake for 15 minutes, then rotate the tray (sheet) and reduce the oven temperature to 160°C/325°F/gas mark 3. Bake for 10–15 minutes more, until the top is dark golden brown and, when you tap the base, it sounds hollow.

Serve warm from the oven, breaking up as required. This keeps for about 4 days, though warm it up before eating. It freezes well for at least 1 month.

For the butter, place the ingredients in a bowl and whisk until smooth and a light cream colour. Scoop out on to baking parchment and roll into a cylinder. Refrigerate until needed, or freeze for a bit if it's very soft, then transfer to the fridge. Store leftovers in the fridge, or freeze for another time.

Variations: For blueberry scones, add 125g (4½oz / scant 1 cup) berries after the dates. Bake for 15 minutes at 200°C/400°F/gas mark 6, rotate the tray (sheet), reduce the oven temperature to 160°C/325°F/gas mark 3 and bake for 15 minutes.

I love this with figs instead of dates, though raisins, sultanas (golden raisins) or dried apricots – maybe with a combination of nuts or seeds – would be great, too.

For a dairy-free vegan loaf, replace the butter with virgin coconut oil and the buttermilk with plant-based milk combined with 1 tsp apple cider vinegar. For glazing, use your chosen milk. It will be flatter but taste great, with a light texture.

Barley malt tea loaf with prunes, dates and raisins

I love this little loaf, densely packed with treacly dried fruits soaked in black tea so that they are extra plump, making each slice incredibly soft and squidgy. The barley malt extract and wholegrain flour combined create the most delicious, rich depth of flavour, while the extra layer of brushed-on malt extract gives the crust a lovely stickiness. It's gorgeous warm from the oven, spread thick with butter.

This is great for breakfast, with tea in the afternoon, or even packed into lunchboxes. When it's a few days old, it's lovely toasted, too.

Barley malt extract can be bought in most health food stores, or online.

SERVES 6–8

unsalted butter or virgin coconut oil or extra virgin cold-pressed rapeseed (canola) oil, for the tin (pan)
100g (3½oz / generous ⅓ cup) boiling water
1 black tea bag
50g (1¾oz / generous ⅓ cup) pitted prunes, chopped into pea-sized pieces
50g (1¾oz / generous ⅓ cup) pitted dates, chopped
50g (1¾oz / scant ⅓ cup) raisins
40g (1½oz / scant ½ cup) light brown muscovado or coconut sugar
1 tbsp molasses
80g (2¾oz / ½ cup) barley malt extract, plus about 2 tbsp more to finish, or as needed
120g (4¼oz / scant 1 cup) wholegrain wheat flour
½ tsp baking powder
pinch of sea salt flakes, crushed
1 egg

Preheat the oven to 160°C/325°F/gas mark 3. Butter or oil the base and sides of a 16 x 9 x 6cm (6¼ x 3½ x 2½in) loaf tin (pan) and line it with baking parchment.

Pour the boiling water into a bowl, add the tea bag, stir, then add the prunes, dates and raisins. Leave to soak while you carry on with the rest of the loaf.

In a small saucepan, warm the sugar, molasses and malt extract over a medium heat until the sugar dissolves, stirring a little with a wooden spoon. Using a whisk, separately combine the flour, baking powder and salt in a bowl. Make a well in the centre, crack in the egg and give it a quick stir in.

Remove the tea bag from the soaked fruits, squeezing out the remaining liquid so that none is lost. Pour the warm malt and sugar mixture into the flour and egg mix, together with the fruit and tea, and fold until well combined. Pour into the prepared tin (pan) and bake for 40 minutes, rotating halfway through baking, or until a skewer inserted in the centre comes out clean and the top, when lightly pressed, bounces back slightly. Remove from the oven and leave to cool for 10 minutes.

Warm the 2 tbsp barley malt extract over a low heat. Remove the loaf from the tin (pan) and brush all the sides, bottom and top with the warmed barley malt extract, using a pastry brush, warming and brushing over a little more if needed. Leave to cool a little longer, then enjoy while still warm.

Store the malt loaf in an airtight container or bag in the fridge for up to 1 week. It freezes well, too, for at least 1 month.

Variation: This is also wonderful baked in slices like a bread and butter pudding. Follow the method for Crema Catalana bread and butter pudding (see page 161), replacing the sourdough with a-few-days-old buttered malt loaf. (And leave out the spices and citrus rind from the custard, if you prefer.)

Spiced orange, apricot and cranberry buns

A bit like a hot cross bun and a little like a tea cake, with wholegrain flour bringing extra depth of flavour, these are lovely. The soft orange-spiced dough is bejewelled with juicy cranberries and apricots and a burst of marmalade. They're not too sweet, so the pink glaze is a yummy, sticky, lick-your-fingers finishing touch. I prefer to use unsulphured apricots, as they have a richer quality.

MAKES 10

150g (5½oz / ⅔ cup) whole milk
25g (1oz / 2 tbsp) unsalted butter
125g (4½oz / scant 1 cup) strong white
  wheat flour, plus more to dust
125g (4½oz / scant 1 cup) strong
  wholegrain wheat flour
40g (1½oz / scant ¼ cup) light brown
  muscovado or coconut sugar
½ tsp sea salt flakes
4g (⅛oz) dried yeast
90g (3¼oz / ¾ cup) dried cranberries
90g (3¼oz / ⅔ cup) dried apricots,
  preferably unsulphured, chopped into
  pea-sized pieces
finely grated zest of 1 orange
¾ tsp ground cinnamon
¾ tsp ground mixed spice (pumpkin
  pie spice)
1 small egg
65g (2¾oz / scant ½ cup) grated apple
extra virgin cold-pressed rapeseed
  (canola) oil, to handle the dough
50g (1¾oz / scant ¼ cup) marmalade,
  plus 10 tsp
20g (¾oz / 4 tsp) water
1 tsp brandy
8 tbsp golden icing (confectioners') sugar
2 tsp orange juice
2 tsp beetroot (beet) juice

Bring the milk just to the boil, add the butter to melt slowly, then let it cool to blood temperature. Mix the flours, sugar, salt, yeast, dried fruits, orange zest and spices in a bowl. Lightly beat the egg and add it to the mix, with the warmed milk and butter (don't worry if the butter hasn't completely melted, it just needs to be soft) and mix by hand to form a soft, sticky dough. Add the apple, mix to incorporate and then turn out on to a well-floured surface.

Knead the dough for about 5 minutes until smooth; it will be sticky because of the fruit, so if you need to re-flour the work surface, do so. After 5 minutes, it will still be a bit sticky, but as long as it feels strong and smooth, it will be fine. (You can also do this in a freestanding mixer fitted with a dough hook.) Be generous with the flour when kneading; you can use up to 60g (2oz). Shape into a ball and place in a clean oiled bowl for about 1½ hours. The dough will not double in size, but it should feel light and rise a little.

Divide into 10 x 75g (2¾oz) pieces. Roll each piece into a ball, then pat it out to about 1cm (½in) thick. Place 1 tsp marmalade in the centre of each round, pinch the dough up around it, turn over and roll until tight. Arrange on a baking tray (sheet) lined with baking parchment, leaving about 3cm (1¼in) between each so they don't stick together. Prove for another hour; they won't double in size due to the amount of fruit, but need to rise a little.

Preheat the oven to 210°C/410°F/gas mark 6½. Put the buns in the oven, reduce the oven temperature to 200°C/400°F/gas mark 6 and bake for 10 minutes. Rotate the tray, reduce the oven temperature to 180°C/350°F/gas mark 4 and bake for a further 10 minutes, until the buns are golden brown and sound hollow when tapped on the bottom. Boil together the 50g (1¾oz) of marmalade, the water and brandy to form a syrup. Reserving some of the pieces of orange rind, brush the buns all over with the syrup. Leave to cool.

Mix together the icing sugar, orange juice and beetroot juice. When the buns are cool, spoon over the pink glaze, letting it fall over the edges. Top each with a few pieces of the reserved orange rind. They're delicious eaten warm. When they're less fresh, toast them and spread with butter and marmalade.

Variation: For hot cross buns, replace the apricots and cranberries with currants, raisins, sultanas (golden raisins) and candied peel and leave out the marmalade centre. For the crosses, mix 80g (2¾oz / ½ cup) plain (all-purpose) flour with enough water to form a thick paste. After the final prove, pipe crosses over the buns and bake as instructed.

CHAPTER 3

CAKES & BISCUITS (COOKIES)

Here, the versatility of natural foods really start to show off, as my magic ingredients join the core flours, sweeteners and fats. A blend of rich brown teff and brown rice flours with caramel-toned coconut or muscovado sugar enhance a light but robustly flavoured cappuccio cake with whipped mascarpone coffee cream; or nutty wholegrain spelt flour, woody maple syrup and velvety rapeseed (canola) oil complement earthy notes in a carrot, beetroot (beet), parsnip and apricot cake with honey-yogurt frosting.

Then there's a flower cake made with lighter white spelt flour and golden caster (superfine) sugar to allow the delicate elderflower and rose to sing; robust barley and wholegrain spelt flours in rooibos fig rolls to complement the fig centre; and molasses adding depth to a crumbly date and oat slice with cardamom and orange.

And there are wonderful textures, from grains such as jumbo oats and oat bran to flakes, buckwheat groats and puffed rice. Crumbly biscuits (cookies), crunchy biscuits (cookies); sponge cakes, brownies, tray bakes and layer cakes. The list goes on… and it's all delicious!

Flower cake

In mid- to late-May, the elderflowers and the roses bloom; both their fragrances intoxicating. In this cake, I really wanted these natural scents to sing, so I've used light base ingredients – white spelt flour and golden caster (superfine) sugar – to make a simple sponge cake, infused with elderflower syrup, then filled with rose petal jelly and whipped elderflower cream. When I can, I make my own jelly and cordial, but good-quality bought versions work just as well. Finish the cake with edible flowers or petals if you can, such as roses, elderflowers, cornflowers, primroses, dianthus, marigolds and pansies.

SERVES 10

170g (6oz / ¾ cup / 1½ sticks) unsalted butter, softened, plus more for the tin (pan)
140g (5oz / scant ¾ cup) golden caster (superfine) sugar
120g (4¼oz / ½ cup) elderflower cordial
170g (6oz / 1¼ cups) white spelt flour
2 tsp baking powder
3 eggs
350g (12oz / 1½ cups) double (heavy) cream
125g (4½oz / scant ½ cup) rose petal jelly, or strawberry jam
edible flowers and petals, to decorate (optional)

Preheat the oven to 180°C/350°F/gas mark 4. Butter the sides and base of a 20cm (8in) loose-bottomed cake tin (pan). Line the base with baking parchment.

In a freestanding mixer fitted with a paddle, or using an electric hand whisk, or by hand, cream the butter, sugar and 30g (1oz / 2 tbsp) of the cordial until light and fluffy, stopping the mixer now and again and scraping everything off the bottom of the bowl once during this time.

Separately whisk together the flour and baking powder. Now return to the butter mixture. While mixing, add 1 egg at a time to the creamed butter and sugar, alternating each addition with one-third of the flour mixture, finishing with the last one-third of the flour mixture. As soon as the batter comes together and looks smooth, stop.

Turn the batter out into the prepared tin (pan) and bake for 25–30 minutes, rotating the cake halfway through, or until the top is golden brown and a skewer inserted in the centre comes out clean.

Remove the cake from the oven, pierce it all over with a skewer, then pour over 60g (2oz / ¼ cup) of the cordial. Leave to cool on a wire rack.

Whip the cream to soft peaks and fold in the remaining 30g (1oz / 2 tbsp) elderflower cordial. Once the cake has cooled, cut it in half horizontally, then fill with the rose petal jelly and half the cream. Put the top on and finish with the remaining cream. Decorate with edible flowers such as rose petals or elderflowers, if you like.

Keep any leftover cake in the fridge for about 5 days, letting it return to room temperature before serving.

Orange, buckwheat and olive oil cake with marmalade syrup

The combination of the buckwheat flour and coconut sugar here create an incredibly nutty, caramel-like, deep richness. The sponge, saturated with a sweet Grand Marnier-spiked marmalade syrup and made with olive oil that keeps it soft and light, is surrounded by finely sliced circles of orange. These become soft and sweet in the oven, while the rinds of the outermost circles get a little burnt and crunchy. The merging of the bittersweet flavours and gorgeous textures is quite divine. It's also very pretty, with the oranges forming a petal pattern around the edge of the cake. I love to serve this warm from the oven, with crème fraîche.

SERVES 10–12

180g (6oz / ¾ cup) extra virgin olive oil, plus more for the tin (pan)
120g (4¼oz / ⅓ cup) honey
200g (7oz / generous ¾ cup) orange juice
about 3 oranges, 550g (1lb 4oz) total weight, plus the finely grated zest of 1 more orange
120g (4¼oz / generous ½ cup) coconut sugar
3 eggs, lightly beaten
90g (3¼oz / scant 1 cup) ground almonds
90g (3¼oz / ⅔ cup) buckwheat flour
1 tsp baking powder
150g (5½oz / ½ cup) marmalade
3 tbsp Grand Marnier, or hazelnut liqueur, or other orange, hazelnut or almond liqueur

Preheat the oven to 180°C/350°F/gas mark 4. Oil a 23cm (9in) loose-bottomed cake tin (pan), then line it with baking parchment, allowing the parchment to slightly come up the edges of the tin (pan), so the juices don't leak when baking.

In a saucepan, bring the honey and orange juice to the boil, then reduce the heat slightly and simmer for 3 minutes to reduce. Turn off the heat. Cut the 550g (1lb 4oz) oranges into thin, 2–3mm (⅛in) slices, discarding the ends, and add to the syrup. Return to a medium boil for 5 minutes, then remove from the heat.

Once cooled a little, arrange the orange slices in the prepared tin (pan), starting from the edges, overlapping the oranges in a circle, then working into the centre of the tin (pan). Once the bottom is covered, start to arrange the slices (again, overlapping them), up the sides of the tin (pan). Cover with 150g (5½oz / ½ cup) of the honey and orange juice mix, leaving the rest in the pan.

In a bowl, whisk the oil with the orange zest, sugar, eggs, ground almonds, flour and baking powder. Pour over the orange slices and syrup and bake for 40 minutes, rotating halfway through, until the top is dark golden brown, firm to the touch and a skewer inserted in the centre comes out clean.

While the cake is baking, add the marmalade to the remaining honey and orange juice in the saucepan, trying to get about equal quantities of the more jammy parts and rindy parts of the marmalade out of the jar. Bring to the boil, then reduce the heat and simmer for a few minutes. Stir in the liqueur, then turn off the heat. When the cake is ready, remove it from the oven, pierce it all over with a skewer, then pour over the marmalade syrup. Leave to cool for about 30 minutes, then remove from the tin (pan) (the orange slices should be lining the bottom and sides) and serve warm, with crème fraîche.

Store in the fridge for 5 days, or freeze for at least 1 month.

Variation: When they are in season (in late winter), I like to use 2 small blood oranges and 2 Jaffa oranges for the orange slices here.

Polenta, kefir, coconut, raspberry and lemon cake with raspberry ripple yogurt cream

This is one big and beautiful show-stopper of a cake. It's a bit like an Eton Mess, but in cake form! I must say, it's one of my favourite recipes in the book; serve it in the late summer when raspberries are at their sweet peak. The subtle, creamy sponge is the perfect canvas on to which raspberries can burst and lemon zing. The three butter-soft layers, with a little texture from the polenta (cornmeal) and vanilla-ish coconut, become moist and sublimely delicious as the juices from the berries sink in. Greek-style yogurt is the perfect addition to the cream, its sharpness balancing out the sweetness of the cake and keeping the filling and topping fresh and light.

SERVES 12–14

For the cake
unsalted butter, for the tins (pans)
90g (3¼oz / ⅔ cup) quick cook polenta (cornmeal)
90g (3¼oz / ⅔ cup) brown rice flour
60g (2oz / ¾ cup) desiccated (dried unsweetened) coconut
240g (8½oz / 1¼ cups) golden caster (superfine) sugar
1½ tsp baking powder
finely grated zest of 2 unwaxed lemons
pinch of sea salt flakes
375g (13oz / 1½ cups) kefir, buttermilk or natural yogurt
135g (4¾oz / ⅔ cup) virgin coconut oil, melted
3 eggs, lightly beaten
375g (13oz / 3 cups) raspberries, fresh or frozen

For the cream
350g (12oz / 1½ cups) double (heavy) cream
350g (12oz / 1½ cups) Greek-style yogurt, the thickest you can find
finely grated zest of 1 unwaxed lemon, plus 1 tbsp lemon juice
3 tbsp golden icing (confectioners') sugar
300g (10½oz / 2½ cups) fresh raspberries, plus more to serve

Preheat the oven to 180°C/350°F/gas mark 4. Butter the sides and bases of 3 x 20cm (8in) loose-bottomed cake tins (pans). Line the bases with baking parchment.

In a bowl, mix together the polenta (cornmeal), rice flour, coconut, sugar, baking powder, lemon zest and salt, using a whisk to disperse all the ingredients evenly. Separately combine the kefir or buttermilk or yogurt, coconut oil and eggs, then mix them into the dry ingredients. Finally, fold in the raspberries, treating the mix as lightly as possible to keep them whole.

Divide the mix between the 3 tins (pans), using about 500g (1lb 2oz) in each tin (pan). Smooth out the tops with a step or cranked palette knife, or the back of a spoon.

Bake for 15 minutes, rotate the tins (pans) and bake for a further 10–15 minutes, or until the tops are golden brown and a skewer inserted in the centre of one of the cakes comes out clean. Leave to cool. They can be frozen at this stage for up to 1 month.

Whip the cream until soft peaks form. Fold in the yogurt, lemon zest and juice and icing (confectioners') sugar. Finally, fold in the raspberries.

Build the cake by spreading each layer with one-third of the cream, trying to top the stack with the most attractive sponge. Finish with extra raspberries (plus their leaves, if you have them) and serve.

Store any leftovers in the fridge for up to 5 days.

Cappuccio cake with whipped mascarpone coffee cream

I discovered brown teff flour a few years ago, made from the seeds of a grass native to Ethiopia and Eritrea. It has a distinct molasses taste. It's lovely with strong flavours such as coffee, dark chocolate and autumn (fall) and winter fruits. Here I combine it with nutty-flavoured brown rice flour (also naturally gluten-free), and together they give a light-as-a-feather crumb with a great depth of flavour, moist with a sweet coffee syrup, between unctuous whipped mascarpone coffee cream layers. Its heavenly delicacy reminds me of the endless frothy-light, creamy cappuccinos – or *cappuccios*, as the locals call them – that I drank every morning when I lived in Bologna. This is a basic sponge mix so, if gluten is not a problem for you, white spelt or wheat flour – or a 50 : 50 blend with wholegrain flour – should work in place of rice and teff flours.

SERVES 10–12

For the coffee
9 tbsp ground coffee

For the cake
180g (6oz / ¾ cup / 1½ sticks) unsalted butter, softened, plus more for the tins (pans)
100g (3½oz / ¾ cup) walnuts
90g (3¼oz / scant ½ cup) light brown muscovado or coconut sugar
90g (3¼oz / scant ¼ cup) dark brown muscovado sugar
50g (1¾oz / scant ¼ cup) coffee
1 tsp vanilla extract
90g (3¼oz / ⅔ cup) brown rice flour
90g (3¼oz / ⅔ cup) brown teff flour
2 tsp baking powder
pinch of sea salt flakes
3 eggs, lightly beaten

For the syrup
50g (1¾oz / scant ¼ cup) coffee
2 tsp maple syrup
2 tsp Tia Maria or Baileys Irish Cream

For the cream
120g (4¼oz / ½ cup) double (heavy) cream
50g (1¾oz / scant ¼ cup) coffee
500g (1lb 2oz / 2¼ cups) mascarpone cheese
3 tbsp maple syrup

Put the ground coffee in a jug (pitcher), pour over 240g (8½oz / 1 cup) boiling water and leave for about 3 minutes. Strain to get 150g (5½oz / ⅔ cup) of coffee. This is the coffee to use in the cake, syrup and cream.

Preheat the oven to 180°C/350°F/gas mark 4. Butter the base and sides of 2 x 18cm (7in) loose-based sandwich tins (pans), then line the bases with baking parchment.

Combine all the syrup ingredients and set aside.

On a baking tray (sheet), lightly toast the walnuts for 5–8 minutes, until smelling toasted, leave to cool, then chop into small pea-sized pieces.

In a freestanding mixer fitted with a paddle, or by hand, cream together the butter and sugars until pale and fluffy. Add the coffee and the vanilla. In a bowl, lightly whisk the flours, baking powder and salt and add the walnuts.

While mixing the butter and sugar, alternately and gradually add the eggs and flours. Mix to just combine, then divide between the prepared tins (pans).

Bake for about 15 minutes, checking after 10 minutes, until a skewer inserted into the centre of the sponges comes out clean and they spring back when lightly touched. Pierce the cakes all over with a skewer and brush over the syrup, distributing it evenly between both. Leave to cool on a wire rack.

Meanwhile, whip the cream to soft peaks, then lightly whisk in the remaining ingredients until smooth, making sure not to over-whip.

Once the cakes are cool, remove them from their tins (pans). Using a cranked or step palette knife or a regular knife, spread half the cream over the bottom sponge. Place the second sponge on top and finish with the remaining cream.

This keeps well for up to 5 days in the fridge. The sponges can also be frozen, without the cream, for up to 1 month.

Carrot, beetroot (beet), parsnip and apricot cake with honey-yogurt frosting

The bright orange, pinks and reds of root vegetables, along with their delicious distinct flavours, always perk me up. I love roasting them, using them in soup and grating them into salads or slaws, and they're wonderful in cakes and desserts, too. The sweet earthy flavour that the root vegetables add to this cake – along with keeping it deliciously soft – is quite divine, working wonderfully with the wholesome spelt flour and flavourful rapeseed (canola) oil. The dried apricots add a little chew, while pumpkin seeds give crunch. The creamy, slightly tangy and fresh-tasting yogurt frosting rounds it all off perfectly.

You will have to start the frosting the day before, to give the yogurt time to drain, though, if you can't, 150g (5½oz) non-strained Greek-style yogurt will also work (but the frosting will be a little looser).

SERVES 8–12

For the frosting
300g (10½oz / 1¼ cups) Greek-style
   yogurt
150g (5½oz / ⅔ cup) cream cheese, at
   room temperature
25g (1oz / 2 tbsp) runny honey
½ tsp vanilla extract
1½ tsp lemon juice
finely grated zest of ¼ large orange
edible flowers or petals, to decorate
   (optional)

For the cake
70g (2½oz / generous ¼ cup) extra virgin
   cold-pressed rapeseed (canola) oil, plus
   more for the tin (pan)
100g (3½oz / generous 1 cup) grated
   carrot
100g (3½oz / generous 1 cup) grated
   beetroot (beet)
100g (3½oz / generous 1 cup) grated
   parsnip
120g (4¼oz / ½ cup) maple syrup
2 eggs, lightly beaten
finely grated zest of ¾ large orange
150g (5½oz / 1⅓ cups) wholegrain
   spelt flour
pinch of sea salt flakes
pinch of mixed spice (pumpkin pie spice)
1 tsp baking powder
60g (2oz / scant ½ cup) dried apricots,
   preferably unsulphured, chopped
40g (1½oz / ¼ cup) pumpkin seeds,
   plus more to decorate

The day before, place the yogurt in a sieve lined with muslin (cheesecloth) or a clean J-cloth, place over a bowl and leave it to strain in the fridge overnight, or for 8–10 hours.

The next day, preheat the oven to 180°C/350°F/gas mark 4. Oil the base and sides of an 18cm (7in) loose-bottomed cake tin (pan), then line the base with baking parchment.

In a bowl, mix together the grated vegetables, maple syrup, eggs, rapeseed (canola) oil and orange zest. In another bowl, combine the flour, salt, mixed spice and baking powder, chopped apricots and pumpkin seeds, then fold them into the wet ingredients until well combined.

Pour into the prepared tin (pan) and bake for 35–40 minutes, turning the cake tin (pan) after 20 minutes, until the top is a light pink-orange golden brown, firm to the touch, bounces back when pressed slightly and a skewer inserted in the centre comes out clean. Leave to cool in the tin (pan).

In a bowl, whisk together the strained yogurt with the rest of the frosting ingredients until completely smooth. Refrigerate until needed.

When the cake is cool, remove it from the tin (pan), transfer to a plate or cake stand and finish with the frosting, smoothing it over with a small cranked or step palette knife or the back of a spoon. Top with more pumpkin seeds and fresh or dried flowers or petals such as tagetes, marigolds and geraniums, if you like.

This cake keeps well for a good 5 days in an airtight container in the fridge. You can also freeze the baked cake, without the frosting, for at least 1 month.

Red wine and cassia poached pear cake

When poached pears are served for dessert, in all their syrupy, spiced glory, you know that winter has arrived. In this cake, I submerge the ruby beauties in a hazelnut and teff flour sponge, the rich notes of the nuts and flour really complementing the red wine fruits. Ground almonds keep the sponge soft. After poaching, I reduce the juices to a heady syrup. Pour it over slices of the cake, top with a spoonful of crème fraîche, thick yogurt or cream, and everyone will be very happy.

Cassia is a beautiful, warm, sweet spice a bit like cinnamon but more intense. It really lifts the flavours, but you can use just 1 tsp if you like your spice more subtle. Most health food shops stock it and it can be found online. Replace it with cinnamon if you cannot find it.

And if you want a richer and stronger tasting syrup to serve alongside, take out the water from the poached pears and just use a whole bottle of wine (about 750g / 1lb 10oz / generous 3 cups).

SERVES 8–10

For the poached pears
500g (1lb 2oz / 2 cups) red wine
  (or see recipe introduction)
200g (7oz / generous ¾ cup) water
120g (4¼oz / generous ½ cup) light
  brown muscovado or coconut sugar
1 cinnamon stick
1 vanilla pod (bean), split lengthways,
  seeds scraped out
3 star anise
5 firm pears, about 700g (1lb 9oz) total
  weight, peeled and kept whole with
  stalks intact (I use Conference)

For the cake
150g (5½oz / ⅔ cup / 1¼ sticks) unsalted
  butter or coconut butter, plus more for
  the tin (pan)
90g (3¼oz / ⅔ cup) hazelnuts
120g (4¼oz / generous ½ cup) light
  brown muscovado or coconut sugar
2 tsp ground cassia (see recipe
  introduction)
150g (5½oz / 1½ cups) ground almonds
75g (2¾oz / ¾ cup) brown teff flour
2 tsp baking powder
½ tsp sea salt flakes
3 eggs, lightly beaten

Poach the pears: place all the ingredients, except the pears, in a wide saucepan – including the empty vanilla pod (bean) – and bring to the boil. Drop in the pears and reduce the heat to a simmer. Cover with the lid or a cartouche – a round of baking parchment cut to fit the pan and touch the surface of the liquid – and cook for 25 minutes, or until the pears are just soft but still a little firm. If they are not completely covered, make sure they are submerged for just over 12 minutes on each side. Turn off the heat and leave covered.

Preheat the oven to 180°C/350°F/gas mark 4. Line a baking tray (sheet) with baking parchment. Butter or oil the base and sides of a 20cm (8in) loose-bottomed cake tin (pan) and line the base with baking parchment.

Toast the hazelnuts on the baking tray (sheet) for 5 minutes, then leave them to cool and grind in a food processor until fine. Combine the ground hazelnuts, sugar, cassia, ground almonds, teff flour, baking powder and salt. Melt the butter and add to the mix with the eggs. Mix until well combined. Pour into the prepared tin (pan). Place the pears on top in a circle, on a slant so they are poking out a little, and slightly overlapping. The stalks and a little of the tops of the fruits should be visible.

Bake for 20 minutes, then rotate the tin (pan) and bake for a further 20 minutes, until just firm to the touch and a skewer inserted in the centre comes out clean. Leave to cool on a wire rack.

Boil the poaching syrup to reduce by half and serve with the warm cake, with crème fraîche, natural yogurt, cream or ice cream. Keep any leftovers in the fridge for up to 5 days, warming them up a little before serving, if you like. Although you may not think it, this also freezes well for up to 1 month.

Fig, banana and dark chocolate cake
with cocoa cream

I love experimenting with vegan baking and it's great to know about egg alternatives that work well, especially if you're suddenly out of eggs. In this recipe, milled flaxseeds mixed with water replace the egg, acting as a binding gel and bringing moisture to the cake. It's a wonderfully wholesome, nourishing, totally lip-smacking recipe: soft banana sponge, crunchy chunks of chocolate and juicy figs, finished with a rich but light ganache-type icing. Children and adults love it, and it's just as good with or without the cream.

SERVES 8–10

For the cake
60g (2oz / scant ⅓ cup) virgin coconut oil, melted, plus more for the tin (pan)
1 tbsp milled flaxseeds (linseeds)
100g (3½oz / scant ½ cup) unsweetened almond milk, or any plant-based milk
1 tsp apple cider vinegar
200g (7oz / ⅔ cup) dried figs, stalks removed, roughly chopped
200g (7oz / generous ¾ cup) water
1¼ tsp bicarbonate of soda (baking soda)
150g (5½oz / 1⅓ cups) wholegrain spelt flour
¼ tsp baking powder
½ tsp sea salt flakes
¼ tsp ground cinnamon
½ tsp ground cardamom
½ tsp mixed spice (pumpkin pie spice)
250g (9oz) banana flesh (about 2 large, ripe bananas)
50g (1¾oz) Apple purée (see page 102)
1 tsp vanilla extract
100g (3½oz) 85% cocoa solids dark chocolate
edible flowers, such as geraniums, to decorate (optional)

For the cocoa cream
125g (4½oz / ½ cup) maple syrup
80g (2¾oz / ¾ cup) cocoa or cacao powder
120g (4¼oz / ½ cup) unsweetened almond milk, or any other plant-based milk
1 tsp vanilla extract
80g (2¾oz / scant ½ cup) virgin coconut oil, melted
pinch of sea salt flakes

Preheat the oven to 180°C/350°F/gas mark 4. Oil the base and sides of a 18cm (7in) loose-bottomed tin (pan) and line the base with baking parchment. Mix together the flaxseeds (linseeds) and 3 tbsp of water and leave for 15 minutes to form a gel. Combine the almond milk with the vinegar and set aside.

In a saucepan, cover the chopped figs with the 200g (7oz / generous ¾ cup) water and bring to the boil. Reduce the heat to a medium boil and cook until the water has evaporated and the figs are soft. Remove from the heat and add ½ tsp of the bicarbonate of soda (baking soda), mashing to form a lumpy figgy paste. Set aside to cool slightly. Separately weigh out the dry ingredients from the spelt flour to the mixed spice, including the remaining ¾ tsp of bicarbonate of soda (baking soda), dispersing any lumps with a whisk.

In a large bowl, mash the bananas, Apple purée, coconut oil and vanilla. Chop the chocolate into pea-sized pieces and add, with the flaxseed (linseed) gel, the milk mix and the flour. Fold in the figs to just combine, working quickly so the chocolate does not melt. Transfer to the prepared tin (pan).

Bake for 30 minutes, then reduce the oven temperature to 160°C/325°F/gas mark 3 and bake for a further 10–12 minutes, or until a skewer inserted in the centre comes out just clean. The top of the cake should be golden brown. Leave to cool in the tin (pan) completely. (If you are leaving off the cream, leave to cool for 10 minutes in the tin / pan, then enjoy while still warm.)

For the cocoa cream, place the ingredients in a blender (or use a hand-held blender) and process until smooth. Place in a bowl, cover with cling film (plastic wrap) and keep in a cool place until the cake has completely cooled and the cream has set (put it in the fridge if it's taking a while). Spread over the cake and top with edible flowers, if you like. This keeps well in a sealed container in the fridge for at least 5 days, or freeze for at least 1 month.

Variations: Sometimes I add chopped toasted walnuts, pecans or hazelnuts, or a mixture, to the batter with the chocolate (add up to 90g / 3¼oz / ¾ cup).

To bake small loaf cakes, preheat the oven to 180°C/350°F/gas mark 4 and bake for 10 minutes, rotate the tin (pan) and bake for 7 minutes, or until a skewer inserted in the centre of a cake comes out clean and the tops are golden brown.

Sticky pear, ginger and molasses cake

I'll never tire of using ground almonds in cakes, their slight oiliness making for a dense stickiness here, with juicy pears tucked between layers of the lovely moist sponge. The strong and distinct sweetness of the dates and molasses, with the soft fruity sweetness of the pears, complement the fiery ginger beautifully. Serve for tea or dessert, with natural yogurt and a drizzle of honey. I like to use Comice or Conference pears for this. To prepare the fresh root ginger, peel and grate. I then slice the grated ginger with a serrated knife so the pieces of ginger fibre in the cake are not too long. You want 60g (2oz / ½ cup) in total, grated and sliced weight, with juices.

SERVES 10

40g (1½oz / scant ¼ cup) extra virgin cold-pressed rapeseed (canola) oil, plus more for the tin (pan)
200g (7oz / 1½ cups) pitted dates
80g (2¾oz / ¼ cup) molasses
120g (4¼oz / ½ cup) natural yogurt
2 eggs, lightly beaten
60g (2oz / ½ cup) peeled and grated fresh root ginger (see recipe introduction)
200g (7oz / 2 cups) ground almonds
pinch of sea salt flakes
1½ tsp baking powder
2 large firm pears, about 350g (12oz) total weight, each peeled, cored and cut into 12 x 1cm (½in) slices

Preheat the oven to 180°C/350°F/gas mark 4. Oil a 20cm (8in) square cake tin (pan), loose-bottomed if possible, and line the base and sides with baking parchment.

In a bowl, cover the dates with the molasses, rapeseed (canola) oil, yogurt, eggs and ginger. Stir together and leave for 10 minutes.

Pour the date mix into a food processor and process until almost smooth, scraping down the mix from the sides of the processor and blending again a few times. Some small lumps of date will be left, which is fine.

Add the ground almonds, salt and baking powder and process once more until smooth.

Pour the batter into the prepared tin (pan), shake the tin slightly to even it out, then arrange the pear slices diagonally on top, slightly pushing them in.

Bake for 40 minutes, rotating the tin (pan) halfway. A dark colour is normal for this cake because of the molasses but, if it's looking very dark, cover with a piece of baking parchment.

Reduce the oven temperature to 150°C/300°F/gas mark 2 and bake for a further 15 minutes, or until the top is firm to the touch. A skewer inserted in the centre will come out almost clean. Leave to cool in the tin (pan) for about 30 minutes, then take it out of the tin (pan).

Serve warm or cold. This will keep well in the fridge for up to 5 days in an airtight container (it's a very moist cake, so it keeps better in the fridge). It will also freeze for up to 1 month.

Chocolate, peanut, rye and raisin brownies

These are totally irresistible, with crunchy toasted peanuts, smooth peanut butter and juicy raisins, all among the most gorgeous dark chocolate goo. The deeply flavoured and softly textured rye flour, the caramel-molasses sweetness of the light and dark brown sugars and the bitter dark chocolate all combine together in the best way possible. Eat alone, or serve with ice cream as a simply perfect end to a meal.

MAKES AT LEAST 16, DEPENDING ON SIZE

100g (3½oz / ½ cup / 1 stick) unsalted butter, plus more for the tin (pan)
80g (2¾oz / generous ½ cup) shelled unsalted peanuts, plus a generous handful for the top
150g (5½oz) 85% cocoa solids dark chocolate, plus 60g (2oz) more for the top, roughly chopped
110g (4oz / generous ½ cup) light brown muscovado or coconut sugar
110g (4oz / generous ½ cup) dark brown muscovado sugar
4 eggs, lightly beaten
1 tsp vanilla extract
70g (2½oz / ⅔ cup) rye flour
1 tsp sea salt flakes
80g (2¾oz / ½ cup) raisins (optional)
150g (5½oz / ⅔ cup) smooth peanut butter

Preheat the oven to 180°C/350°F/gas mark 4. Butter the base and sides of a 20cm (8in) square tin (pan), loose-bottomed if possible, and line it with baking parchment. Line a baking tray (sheet) with baking parchment.

Spread the 80g (2¾oz / generous ½ cup) peanuts on the prepared tray (sheet) and toast them in the oven for about 5 minutes, or until just golden. Remove from the oven to cool.

Melt the butter and chocolate in a heatproof bowl placed over a saucepan of simmering water. Make sure the bowl does not touch the water. Turn off the heat and, with the bowl still over the hot water, add the sugars, eggs and vanilla and mix in, making sure there are no lumps of sugar. Add the flour, salt, raisins, if using, and toasted peanuts and stir to combine, until smooth and glossy. Pour into the prepared tin (pan) and blob the peanut butter over the mix in spoonfuls. Using a small knife or skewer, swirl the peanut butter into the brownie. Top with the 60g (2oz) chopped chocolate, pushing it slightly into the batter, and sprinkle over the extra handful of peanuts. Shake the tin a little to settle the ingredients.

Bake for 10 minutes, then rotate the tin (pan) and bake for a further 5 minutes, or until just set with a little wobble. A skewer inserted into the centre should come out with a little mix on it. Leave to cool slightly, then remove from the tin (pan) and serve warm, while at their gooey best. Cut into 16 squares, or make them smaller if you like, as they are quite rich.

These will keep in an airtight container for up to 5 days in the fridge, or freeze for at least 1 month. They become firmer in the fridge, but the flavours stay fresher. However, if you prefer to keep them softer, keep them out of the fridge. When they are less fresh, they are lovely served warmed through.

Variation: Replace the rye flour with brown teff flour for a gluten-free brownie.

Date and oat slice with cardamom and orange

Boiling the dates in orange juice uplifts their sweetness and keeps the filling moist and juicy. The biscuit (cookie) layer below the dates becomes a little soft, while the top layer gets crumbly-crunchy, with pumpkin seeds adding an extra bite and toasted flavour. The warming cardamom with the sweet orange-plumped dates and the wholesome warmth of the oats all come together wonderfully. Great as a snack, in lunchboxes, or even for breakfast with yogurt.

If you can't find oat flour, blitz up oats in a food processor or blender until they are as fine as possible, to form a flour.

MAKES ABOUT 24 SQUARES, DEPENDING ON SIZE

180g (6oz / ¾ cup / 1½ sticks) unsalted butter, plus more for the tin (pan)
500g (1lb 2oz / 3¾ cups) pitted dates
300g (10½oz / 1¼ cups) water
finely grated zest of 2 oranges, plus 300g (10½oz / 1¼ cups) orange juice
200g (7oz / 1⅓ cups) oat flour (or see recipe introduction)
250g (9oz / 2⅔ cups) rolled oats
½ tsp sea salt flakes
½ tsp bicarbonate of soda (baking soda)
½ tsp ground cinnamon
1½ tsp ground cardamom
4 tbsp milled flaxseeds (linseeds)
60g (2oz / scant ½ cup) pumpkin seeds
100g (3½oz / ½ cup) light brown muscovado or coconut sugar
100g (3½oz / generous ⅓ cup) date syrup

Preheat the oven to 180°C/350°F/gas mark 4. Butter the base and sides of a 30 x 20 x 3cm (12 x 8 x 1¼in) baking tin (pan), then line them with baking parchment, so that it comes over the edges (to easily remove it later).

Place the dates in a saucepan with the water, zest and 200g (7oz / generous ¾ cup) of the juice. Cook over a medium heat, stirring now and again to stop them catching, until the dates are soft, have absorbed the liquids and formed a loose paste. You don't want it to be too dry and you'll need to mash it towards the end to help it along, if the dates being used are on the dry side.

In a bowl, mix together all the dry ingredients from the oat flour to the pumpkin seeds.

In a saucepan, bring the sugar, date syrup, butter and remaining orange juice just to the boil, to melt the butter. Remove from the heat, mix the dry ingredients into the butter and sugar mixture and combine well.

Put 600g (1lb 5oz) of the oat mix into the prepared tin (pan) and spread it out with your fingertips, then even it out using a cranked or step palette knife or the back of a spoon. Spread over the date paste, again using a cranked or step palette knife, or a regular kitchen knife, to even it out. Finish by crumbling over the remaining oat mix, lightly pressing it into the dates.

Bake for 15 minutes, then reduce the oven temperature to 140°C/275°F/gas mark 1, rotate the tin (pan) and bake for a further 8–10 minutes, until the top is golden brown. Leave to cool in the tin (pan).

Remove from the tin (pan) by lifting it out with the baking parchment on to a chopping board, then slice into squares. Store in an airtight container for up to 1 week in the fridge. These freeze well, too, for at least 1 month.

Variation: Try mixed berry flapjacks. Replace the date centre with 400–500g (14oz–1lb 2oz / 2¾–3¼ cups) blueberries, raspberries or blackberries, or a mix, slightly mashed with a little sugar, to taste (not strawberries, they are too watery).

Crumbly hazelnut and dark chocolate *baci*

This recipe is a mixture of a few of my favourite things from Italy: heavenly biscuits called *baci di dama* ('ladies' kisses'), and some lovely chocolates called *baci* ('kisses') with a dark chocolate shell and chunky hazelnut centre. Oat flour has a soft taste, allowing the hazelnut and chocolate, always a winning combination, to really sing; it is also naturally gluten-free, creating the crumbliest dough. These just melt in the mouth. They're dainty and perfect with a cup of tea or coffee, or lovely after supper, too.

If you cannot find oat flour, used rolled oats and process them in a food processor or high-speed blender until they are as fine as possible. Arrowroot is available in most supermarkets and health food shops.

MAKES 18 SANDWICHED BISCUITS (COOKIES)

For the biscuits (cookies)
100g (3½oz / ¾ cup) oat flour (or see recipe introduction)
100g (3½oz / ⅔ cup) blanched hazelnuts, or whole hazelnuts with skins
4 tsp arrowroot powder (this helps to bind the ingredients in this gluten-free dough)
pinch of sea salt flakes
½ tsp baking powder
60g (2oz / generous ¼ cup) light brown muscovado or coconut sugar
40g (1½oz / scant ¼ cup) unsalted butter, softened (or see Variation, right)
100g (3½oz / generous ⅓ cup) hazelnut butter
1 tsp vanilla extract

For the ganache
100g (3½oz) 85% dark chocolate, broken up into small pieces
100g (3½oz / generous ⅓ cup) double (heavy) cream, or whipping cream
1 tbsp Frangelico, or other hazelnut liqueur (optional)

Preheat the oven to 180°C/350°F/gas mark 4. Line a baking tray (sheet) with baking parchment.

Process the oat flour, hazelnuts, arrowroot, salt, baking powder and sugar in a food processor until fine. Add the butter and process to a crumb-like consistency. Add the hazelnut butter and vanilla extract and process until it comes together in a ball. Stop the processor to scrape the mix off the bottom of the bowl if necessary. (It's quite a dry dough.)

Roll into 36 balls, each about 1 tsp in size or 10–12g (¼–½oz), and press each one in the palm of your hand, slightly rolling and forming it to make smooth rounds. Place on the prepared baking tray (sheet), go around the edges with your fingers to neaten them up, then press each biscuit (cookie) gently with a fork. Bake for 8–10 minutes, until light golden brown; the surfaces will have just begun to crack. Leave to cool, while you make the ganache.

Place the chocolate in a small heatproof bowl. Bring the cream just to the boil, add the liqueur, if using, mix, then pour over the chocolate. Stir with a spatula until the chocolate has melted and the ganache is smooth and emulsified. Place a piece of cling film (plastic wrap) directly on the surface of the ganache and leave to firm up in a cool place for about 30 minutes.

Turn half the biscuits (cookies) over so their flat sides are uppermost. When the ganache is set but still soft, using a couple of teaspoons or a piping (pastry) bag, divide it over this half of the biscuits (cookies), spreading it on their flat sides. Place a plain biscuit (cookie) on top to make a sandwich, press a little, then leave to set in a cool place. There will be some ganache left over. It can be used to fill pastry shells for chocolate tarts, to ice cakes, to spoon over ice cream, or even rolled into truffles, coated with cocoa powder. It's also great used a chocolate spread for toast (it stores in the fridge for 1 week).

These keep well for a good 5 days in an airtight container in a cool place. You can also form the biscuits (cookies) and freeze them raw for at least 1 month, then bake them from the freezer, allowing a few extra minutes' baking time.

Variations: You can replace the butter with virgin coconut oil (but make sure to leave the biscuits / cookies to cool completely, as they will be crumblier than the butter version). Sandwich the biscuits (cookies) together with dairy-free ganache (see page 144), if you need these to be vegan.

These are great even without the ganache, with any nut or nut butter swapped in for the hazelnuts used here. Try them with your favourites – peanuts and almonds are mine – or use tahini in place of nut butter and walnuts instead of hazelnuts.

Pistachio, cranberry and cardamom sablés with *fleur de sel*

These delicate biscuits (cookies) are not too sweet, thanks to the low sugar content and the addition of salt, which helps the cardamom to really sing. While the crumbly biscuit (cookie) melts in the mouth, there is the fruity-sweet tang and chewiness from the dried cranberries and a crunch from the outer layer of ground, toasted pistachios. Perfect with a cup of tea after work, or with a fruit compote and ice cream, or served alongside a creamy pudding such as lemon posset.

MAKES 26

100g (3½oz / 1 cup) shelled, unsalted pistachio nuts
290g (10oz / 2½ cups) white spelt or wheat flour
40g (1½oz / ¼ cup) golden icing (confectioners') sugar
30g (1oz / ⅓ cup) cornflour (cornstarch)
½ tsp sea salt flakes or *fleur de sel*, crumbled with your fingers
1 tsp ground cardamom
80g (2¾oz / ¾ cup) dried cranberries
240g (8¾oz / 1 cup / 2¼ sticks) unsalted butter, cold and cut into cubes
1 egg white

Blitz the pistachios in a food processor until fine, but still with a little texture. Set aside.

Combine all the dry ingredients, except the pistachios, in a freestanding mixer fitted with a paddle. Add the cubes of butter and mix until it just comes together. (If you do not have a mixer and are making the dough by hand, it is easier to cream together the butter and icing (confectioners') sugar first, then work in the rest of the dry ingredients, finishing with the cranberries.)

Lift the dough out of the bowl and bring it into a log shape, treating it as lightly as possible. On a piece of baking parchment, shape the dough into a rectangle, about 26cm (10½in) long, 4cm (1½in) deep and 5cm (2in) wide. Roll the baking parchment around it and chill in the fridge or freezer for 30 minutes, or until firm.

Preheat the oven to 160°C/325°F/gas mark 3. Line a baking tray (sheet) with baking parchment.

When the dough is chilled and firm, trim the ends to straighten if necessary. Spread the pistachios out on a wide plate or work surface. Brush the dough lightly with egg white and then roll it through the ground pistachios, pressing them lightly into the dough to make sure they stick and do not come off during baking. Cut the dough to a little thinner than 1cm (½in) pieces and place, 2cm (¾in) apart, on the prepared tray (sheet).

Bake for about 12 minutes, checking after 10, or until the edges are just slightly golden. Leave to cool completely on the tray (sheet), or they will crumble when you pick them up. Eat when cool, or package up for a perfect edible gift. These keep in an airtight container for at least 5 days. The raw dough freezes for at least 1 month, so you don't need to bake it all at once.

Variation: Replace the cranberries with half-and-half roughly chopped pistachio nuts and walnuts for a nuttier, crunchier biscuit (cookie). The crunch of the nuts within the soft, crumbly biscuit (cookie) is divine.

Chunky buckwheat and triple nut brittle

This is a wonderfully simple and quick-to-make recipe that is crunchy, sweet, nutty and very moreish indeed. I wanted to use an array of nuts for their different textures and flavours, with crunchier Brazil nuts and softer, creamier cashews and macadamias, while the buckwheat groats have a distinct, mild and earthy taste and a little bite, too. Snap it up as a snack, have a piece or two with a cup of tea, or it's just delicious served in shards with ice cream or thick yogurt. It's great with Baked bananas with lime and coconut cream (see page 168), too.

SERVES 8–10

20g (¾oz / 4 tsp) virgin coconut oil
130g (4¾oz / ½ cup) maple syrup
1 tsp vanilla extract
80g (2¾oz / ½ cup) buckwheat groats
50g (1¾oz / scant ½ cup) Brazil nuts,
    each roughly chopped into 3–4 pieces
50g (1¾oz / scant ½ cup) macadamia
    nuts, halved
50g (1¾oz / ¼ cup) whole cashew nuts
50g (1¾oz / ⅔ cup) buckwheat flakes,
    oats or other flakes
pinch of sea salt flakes

Preheat the oven to 180°C/350°F/gas mark 4. Line a baking tray (sheet) with a silicone mat (non-stick baking mat) or a piece of baking parchment.

In a saucepan, bring the coconut oil, maple syrup and vanilla just to the boil. Remove from the heat, add the buckwheat groats, all the nuts, buckwheat flakes and salt and stir to combine.

Pour the mix on to the prepared tray (sheet) and spread it out with a cranked or step palette knife until it is no thicker than the halved macadamia nuts. A lot of the nuts will be on the edge, but this is fine; you can lift them up and place them in the centre. Bake for 10 minutes.

Remove from the oven and roughly chop into generous pieces, about 5cm (2in) wide, being careful not to cut the silicone mat (non-stick baking mat), if using. I like to make triangles, but any shape is fine. Return to the oven for 10–13 more minutes until golden brown. Leave to cool on the tray (sheet), so they harden up and set firm.

These will keep for at least 5 days in an airtight jar.

Rooibos and barley fig rolls

The full-bodied flavour of rooibos tea really flatters the rich sweetness of the fig filling in these biscuits (cookies). I always loved fig rolls as a child, but it's such fun to make your own from scratch and they're so much more delicious with those nourishing and tasty wholegrains, which create a great consistency, too. Barley flour gives a bit of extra crunch, while spelt flour keeps it crumbly and soft.

MAKES 20

For the fig filling
2 rooibos tea bags, or 2 tsp loose-leaf
    rooibos tea
240g (8½oz / 2 cups) dried figs, stalks
    removed, roughly chopped
finely grated zest of 1 medium orange,
    plus 80g (2¾oz / ⅓ cup) orange juice
1 tsp vanilla extract
½ tsp ground cinnamon
15g (½oz / 1 tbsp) honey
160g (5¾oz / ⅔ cup) water

For the biscuit (cookie) dough
4 rooibos tea bags, or 4 tsp loose-leaf
    rooibos tea
80g (2¾oz / generous ½ cup) wholegrain
    barley flour, plus more to dust
120g (4¼oz / 1 cup) wholegrain spelt
    flour
70g (2½oz / ⅓ cup) light brown
    muscovado or coconut sugar
pinch of sea salt flakes
finely grated zest of 1 medium orange
100g (3½oz / ½ cup) virgin coconut oil,
    melted
1 tsp vanilla extract

Start by making the filling. If using tea bags, cut them open and empty the contents into a medium-small saucepan. Add the other ingredients and bring to the boil. Cook until the liquids are just absorbed. Remove from the heat and blend with a hand-held blender until relatively smooth. Set aside to cool.

Meanwhile, get on with the biscuit (cookie) dough. In a frying pan (skillet) over a medium heat, empty in the tea from the tea bags (or just spoon in the tea) and toast for 2 minutes, just to release its flavours. When cool, mix it with the flours, sugar, salt and orange zest in a bowl. Add the coconut oil, 1 tbsp water and the vanilla extract and mix until well combined, bringing it together with your hands into a ball.

Flatten the dough out on a lightly floured piece of baking parchment into a rough rectangle. Lightly flour the dough, place a piece of baking parchment on top and roll it out to a 23 x 18cm (9 x 7in) rectangle, using your hands to reshape when necessary. The dough should be a bit less than 5mm (¼in) thick. Transfer to a baking tray (sheet), with the sheet of baking parchment underneath.

Place the cooled fig paste in a cylinder down the middle of the rectangle of dough, leaving a rim of about 6cm (2½in) on either side. Carefully roll the left side of the dough rectangle over the paste, to create a cylinder shape with a flat bottom. The dough might crack a bit on the left side, but that is normal. Refrigerate for 1 hour, or until firmer and easy to cut with a sharp knife.

Preheat the oven to 180°C/350°F/gas mark 4. Line a baking tray (sheet) with baking parchment.

Take the dough out of the fridge. Carefully cut into 1cm- (½in-) thick pieces using a sharp knife (they may crumble a little but that is normal), and place on the prepared tray (sheet). Bake for 30 minutes, turning the rolls over halfway with a spatula, so they colour evenly on both sides. Leave to cool slightly, then serve.

These will keep for up to 5 days in a jar, biscuit (cookie) tin or airtight container, or freeze for up to 1 month. The raw biscuits (cookies) can also be frozen for up to 1 month. Bake from frozen, adding a few minutes to the baking time.

Wholegrain oat bran malty biscuits (cookies)

The oat bran in these adds a lovely little crunch to what is otherwise a simple and delicious, crumbly wholegrain biscuit (cookie). The brown sugar together with a hint of barley malt extract adds just the right amount of malty-caramel sweetness. Yes, they're a little reminiscent of digestives (graham crackers), but I promise, they're a lot yummier and just perfect with a cup of tea after a long day, or packed into lunchboxes. It's great to have this recipe to hand, too, to be used for cheesecake bases or, broken up, in the Tahini honey tiffin with puffed rice and figs (see overleaf).

    Using either muscovado or coconut sugars gives a similar dough. But, once cooked, the biscuits (cookies) with coconut sugar are slightly darker and more cracked, with a deeper taste (the biscuits /cookies in this photograph were made with coconut sugar). The muscovado version are slightly crisper.

MAKES 13–14

135g (4¾oz / 1 cup) wholegrain wheat flour
70g (2½oz / ¾ cup) oat bran
45g (1¾oz / ¼ cup) light brown muscovado or coconut sugar
1 tsp baking powder
pinch of sea salt flakes
90g (3¼oz / ⅓ cup / ¾ stick) unsalted butter, at room temperature, chopped
1 tbsp whole milk
1½ tsp barley malt extract

Place the flour, bran, sugar, baking powder and salt in a food processor and pulse to combine. Add the butter and process once more until the mix resembles crumbs. Finally, add the milk and malt extract and process until the dough just comes together.

Turn out on to a piece of baking parchment, cover with another piece of baking parchment and roll the dough until it is just under 1cm (½in) thick. Refrigerate for 30 minutes.

Preheat the oven to 180°C/350°F/gas mark 4. Line a baking tray (sheet) with baking parchment.

Remove the dough from the fridge and peel off the top layer of baking parchment. Using a 6cm (2½in) biscuit (cookie) cutter, cut out 13–14 biscuits (cookies); you will need to re-roll the dough. Place on the prepared tray (sheet), then pierce each biscuit (cookie) 3 times with a fork. They spread a very small amount when baking, so make sure to leave a few centimetres between each. Bake for 15 minutes, rotating the tray (sheet) after 10 minutes, until golden brown. Leave to cool completely on the tray (sheet).

These will keep well in an airtight container at room temperature for at least 5 days. You can also freeze the raw dough for at least 1 month and bake off the biscuits (cookies) when you need them.

Tahini honey tiffin with puffed rice and figs

After I developed the recipe for the Wholegrain oat bran malty biscuits (cookies) (see page 98), my mind wandered, thinking of all the delicious things to which I could add them to create new and fun recipes. Obviously you can use store-bought digestives (graham crackers) for this recipe, too – Doves Farm sell a good wholegrain version – but if you have time to make your own (they're very quick, I promise!), I would thoroughly recommend it. This is a fun-to-make and very moreish fridge cake comprising a crunchy chocolate base studded with puffed rice and chewy dried figs, finished with a creamy rich layer of dark chocolate and tahini. It's very good with a cup of tea or coffee, in packed lunches, or for dessert with ice cream. In the winter I love to add crystallized (candied) ginger for its Christmassy flavour.

**MAKES ABOUT 20 SQUARES,
DEPENDING ON SIZE**

For the base
100g (3½oz) 70% cocoa solids
   dark chocolate
50g (1¾oz / 3½ tbsp) unsalted butter,
   or virgin coconut oil
1 tbsp honey
70g (2½oz / ⅓ cup) tahini
70g (2½oz) Wholegrain oat bran malty
   biscuits (cookies) (see page 98),
   or wholegrain digestives
   (graham crackers)
70g (2½oz / generous ½ cup) dried figs,
   stalks cut off, roughly chopped
15g (½oz / ½ cup) puffed rice

For the top layer
100g (3½oz) 70% cocoa solids
   dark chocolate, broken up or
   roughly chopped
15g (½oz / 1 tbsp) unsalted butter, or
   virgin coconut oil
1 tsp honey
30g (1oz / scant ¼ cup) tahini

Line the base and sides of a 15 x 10cm (6 x 4in) square tin (pan) with baking parchment. If you have a slightly different-sized tin (pan), it doesn't matter; you just want the tiffin to be about 3cm (1¼in) thick.

Make the base layer by melting the chocolate, butter and honey in a heatproof bowl placed over a saucepan of simmering water (make sure the bowl does not touch the water). Remove from the heat and stir in the tahini. Add the biscuits (cookies), lightly crushing them with your fingers as you do so, making sure to keep some large bits and breaking the rest up into smaller pieces. Now add the figs and puffed rice and stir everything together well. Pour into the prepared tin (pan) and place in the freezer.

Make the top layer by melting the chocolate, butter and honey in a heatproof bowl as before. Remove from the heat, pour over the set base layer, then swirl in the tahini: spoon blobs over the top and swirl them with a skewer or a small sharp knife. Return to the fridge for about 2 more hours, or until set.

Remove from the tin (pan) and cut into squares, whatever size you prefer, with a serrated knife. This will keep for at least 1 week in an airtight container in the fridge. It freezes well, too, for at least 1 month, though the puffed rice will be a little softer after defrosting.

Five-in-one oaty cookie cakes

For the base recipe

135g (4¾oz / ½ cup / 1⅛ sticks) unsalted
   butter, softened
80g (2¾oz / scant ½ cup) light brown
   muscovado or coconut sugar
80g (2¾oz) Apple Purée (see below)
155g (5½oz / generous 1 cup) strong
   wholegrain wheat or spelt flour
100g (3½oz / generous 1 cup) rolled or
   jumbo oats (I like half-and-half)
¼ tsp sea salt flakes
½ tsp bicarbonate of soda (baking soda)
½ tsp vanilla extract
1 egg, lightly beaten

**For dark chocolate chunk, pecan
   nut and fig**

60g (2oz / generous ½ cup) pecan nuts,
   or other nuts of your choice
60g (2oz) 70–85% cocoa solids dark
   chocolate, roughly chopped
60g (2oz / ½ cup) dried figs, stalks
   removed, roughly chopped

**For pistachio nut, white chocolate,
   cranberry and orange blossom**

60g (2oz / ½ cup) pistachio nuts
60g (2oz) white chocolate, chopped
60g (2oz / ½ cup) dried cranberries
finely grated zest of 1 orange
2½ tsp orange blossom water

For oat and raisin

100–120g (3½–4¼oz / ⅔–¾ cup) raisins
½ tsp ground cinnamon
handful of oats, rolled or jumbo,
   to sprinkle

For granola

125g (4½oz / 1 cup) granola
   (for home-made, see page 32),
   plus more to sprinkle

For very berry

up to 200g (7oz / 1½ cups) mixed berries
   (I use blackberries, raspberries
   and blueberries), fresh or frozen

Oats are certainly one of my favourite ingredients for their versatility, creamy taste, great texture and all-round goodness. Don't save them just for breakfast time, as they're lovely added to pastry or even ice cream, or ground and used as a flour in cakes and cookies. These are gorgeously soft and light, a little more cake-like than a regular chewy cookie, but in a very good and delicious way. Use this simple base recipe, then add whatever you like according to the measurements below; I've given five of my favourite versions.

Preheat the oven to 180°C/350°F/gas mark 4. Line a baking tray (sheet) with baking parchment. If making either of the nut versions, tip either the pecan or pistachio nuts on to another tray (sheet) and toast in the oven for 5 minutes. Allow to cool, then roughly chop.

In a freestanding mixer fitted with a paddle, cream the butter, sugar and Apple Purée. It will look a little split. Separately combine the flour, oats, salt and bicarbonate of soda (baking soda). Add the vanilla to the butter, then the egg, then the dry ingredients, still mixing. Add your chosen extras and mix once more. Spoon on to the prepared tray (sheet), making 12 cookies, each 6–7cm (2½in) in diameter. Sprinkle with oats or granola, if using.

Bake for 10 minutes, then rotate the tray (sheet) and bake for 3 minutes, until golden brown but soft to the touch in the centre. Slide on to a wire rack and leave to cool. Keep the cookies in a sealed container or jar for up to 1 week. They freeze well, too.

You don't need to bake all the cookies: freeze the discs of raw dough on a baking tray (sheet), then lift them off and keep in the freezer for at least 1 month. Bake from frozen, adding a few extra minutes to the baking time.

Apple purée

MAKES ABOUT 1KG (2LB 4OZ)

12 apples (each 120–140g / 4¼–5oz), I like Cox apples here

Preheat the oven to 180°C/350°F/gas mark 4. Wash and dry the apples, then cut into quarters. Place on a baking tray (sheet) and bake until soft, 20–30 minutes. Leave to cool slightly and do not discard the liquids. In a blender, blend the cooked apples and juices to a smooth, sweet, thick purée. (If your blender is a bit less powerful than a high-speed blender, do peel and core the apples first.) Either use immediately, keep in the fridge for up to 5 days, or freeze in batches in glass jars or freezer bags for up to 1 month.

This tray, clockwise from this photo: white spelt Poppy seed streusel made with coconut sugar; brown rice and polenta Poppy seed streusel made with light brown muscovado sugar; white spelt Poppy seed streusel made with light brown muscovado sugar

Poppy seed streusel

Streusel is the German word for crumble, often baked on top of cakes, choux pastry buns and sweet breads. You could add this topping to the Red wine and cassia poached pear cake (see page 80), for example, before baking. It can be baked alone, too, as I do here, and eaten as something sweet to nibble on, a bit like chunks of biscuit (cookie). Sprinkle it on ice cream, or on stewed fruits as a last-minute crumble, or just eat it with fresh sliced fruit and cream. I give you two options here: the first with white spelt flour for a softer biscuit (cookie), the other with brown rice and polenta (cornmeal) if you like the extra crunch.

SERVES 6–8

120g (4¼oz / 1 cup) white spelt flour
70g (2½oz / ⅓ cup) light brown muscovado or coconut sugar
75g (2¾oz / ¾ cup) ground almonds
½ tsp baking powder
finely grated zest of ½ unwaxed lemon
pinch of sea salt flakes
30g (1oz / ¼ cup) poppy seeds
80g (2¾oz / ⅓ cup / ¾ stick) cold unsalted butter, cubed
1 egg yolk
½ tsp vanilla extract

Preheat the oven to 150°C/300°F/gas mark 2. Line a baking tray (sheet) with baking parchment.

In a freestanding mixer fitted with a paddle, combine all the ingredients from the flour to the poppy seeds. Add the butter and mix until it resembles crumbs. Combine the egg yolk and vanilla and mix in until just combined. It should look like a crumble, with larger chunks and smaller crumbs.

Turn out on to the prepared tray (sheet), making sure that it is evenly distributed. Bake for 15–20 minutes, or until golden brown and in small to large crumb-like pieces, checking after 10 minutes and moving it around with a spatula just to help the pieces separate and brown evenly. Leave to cool.

Store in a glass jar for up to 1 week. You can also store the raw dough in the freezer for at least 1 month and bake off from the freezer, adding a few more minutes to the baking time.

Varations: For a gluten-free version, replace the white spelt flour with 60g (2oz / ½ cup) brown rice flour and 60g (2oz / generous ⅓ cup) fine, quick cook polenta (cornmeal). Bake as instructed.

Orange zest works well instead of lemon.

Coconut and oat biscuits (cookies) with chocolate and toasted flaked coconut

Whether in porridge (oatmeal), a cake, flapjacks, muesli or sprinkled over a loaf of bread before baking, oats are such a great reliable, filling and versatile ingredient. These are a bit like oatcakes, but made sweeter with maple syrup, coconut and chocolate, the latter two ingredients together being one of my favourite combinations. From the soft crunch of the biscuit (cookie), to the fine snap of the chocolate, topped with the extra crunchy toasted coconut, the textures are all terrific. Dip them in a cup of tea, pack them in lunchboxes, or have them for dessert, crumbled over natural yogurt or ice cream.

MAKES 15

110g (4oz / generous 1 cup) rolled oats
60g (2oz / scant 1 cup) desiccated (dried unsweetened) coconut
pinch of sea salt flakes
20g (¾oz / 4 tsp) virgin coconut oil or unsalted butter, melted
4 tbsp cold water, plus more if needed
25g (1oz / 2 tbsp) maple syrup
1 tbsp vanilla extract
30g (1oz / ½ cup) flaked coconut, unsweetened
100g (3½oz) 70% cocoa solids dark chocolate, broken up or chopped

Preheat the oven to 180°C/350°F/gas mark 4. Line 2 baking trays (sheets) with baking parchment.

In a food processor, process the oats until as fine a flour as possible. Add the desiccated (dried unsweetened) coconut and salt and process to combine.

Add the coconut oil or butter, water, maple syrup and vanilla extract and process once more until the mix comes together, stopping the processor and scraping it down from the sides a few times. Bring the dough together in your hands and place on to a piece of baking parchment, flattening it out a little. Top with another piece of baking parchment and roll out to 5mm (¼in) thick.

Cut out biscuits (cookies) with a 6cm (2½in) round cutter. Press the off-cuts together in your hands and roll out again, adding a splash of water if it is breaking apart. Re-roll and cut out more rounds until you have 15 biscuits (cookies). Transfer to 1 of the prepared trays (sheets) and bake for 12–14 minutes, until the biscuits (cookies) are firm to the touch (they will still look quite pale). Leave to cool on the tray (sheet).

Spread the coconut flakes on the second prepared tray (sheet) and bake in the oven for 3 minutes, or until golden. Transfer to a plate to cool.

Melt the chocolate in a heatproof bowl over a saucepan of simmering water, making sure the bowl does not touch the water. Stir until it has completely melted, then remove from the heat. Carefully dip the top of each cooled biscuit (cookie) in the melted chocolate, return it to the tray (sheet), then cover with toasted coconut flakes, pressing them in lightly to stick. Leave the biscuits (cookies) in the fridge for a few minutes to harden.

Store in an airtight container for up to 5 days. The raw biscuit (cookie) dough will freeze well for at least 1 month, or you can freeze the raw cut-out biscuits (cookies) and bake from frozen, adding a few minutes to the baking time.

CHAPTER 4

LUNCHES & SUPPERS

These recipes allowed me to use even more wonderful ingredients, such as emmer, millet and grain-free chickpea (garbanzo bean) flour. There are also colourful, vibrant vegetables, cheeses, fish and meat, nuts, seeds and grains.

Here, I want to give you a good number of 'base' recipes – pastry (pie crust), flatbread, polenta (cornmeal), pasta and pancakes – on to which you can add what is in season, local, or in your cupboard.

Feel free to change ingredients with the seasons. In winter, roast squash with onions and substitute those for the summer vegetables in the tarte Tatin with pecorino pastry; change or take out the cheese in other recipes if you prefer; or add fish or meat.

Do what you like, make these and all the recipes in this book your own and discover the great adaptability of those gorgeous grains and fresh natural ingredients. And, don't forget, leftovers from supper are always good for lunch the next day.

A *smörgåsbord* of rye tartlets with baked salmon, pickled herring, smoked mackerel…

While studying at Edinburgh University, I lived with a beautiful Swedish friend called Lena. One very cold April, I visited her in Stockholm, and we had a great time enjoying *fika* (coffee and pastries) in all the cosy *bageriet* (bakeries), visiting galleries and museums and keeping our energy levels up with lots of delicious open sandwiches, or *smörgås*, for our lunches. The traditional rye bread used, with its robust flavour, is a great carrier for many toppings; here I've replaced the bread with a 100% dark rye, seeded, crumbly pastry shell. Take these on a summer's picnic, serve them as canapés, or have them for lunch, letting your guests fill them with whatever they like; I give some options below. Build the tartlet fillings from a main ingredient, such as fish, cheese, vegetables, meat or eggs, and always include some kind of moisture in the form of crème fraîche, soured cream, mayonnaise or cream cheese, so the tarts aren't too dry. Pickled and raw vegetables are very good additions and I always like lots of herbs, too. I enjoy the seeds in the pastry (pie crust) for their flavour and contrasting texture, but you can leave them out if you prefer.

Buy sustainably sourced seafood, caught locally if possible.

MAKES 18, DEPENDING ON THE SIZE OF THE TINS (PANS)

For the tartlets
120g (4¼oz / 1 cup) dark rye flour, plus more to dust
½ tsp sea salt flakes
1 tsp fennel seeds
1 tsp caraway seeds
2 tsp each sesame, poppy and golden linseeds (flaxseeds)
60g (2oz / ¼ cup / ½ stick) unsalted butter, cold and cut into cubes, plus more for the tins (pans)
1 egg, lightly beaten

Fillings I love:
smoked mackerel, horseradish cream and radishes
baked or smoked salmon, crème fraîche and dill
pickled herring, soured cream, chives and garlic chive flowers
quail's eggs, prawns (shrimp), cod's roe or caviar

In a freestanding mixer fitted with a paddle, combine the flour, salt and all the seeds with the butter, processing only until the mix resembles crumbs. Add the egg and mix once more until the dough just comes together. If it's a little sticky that's fine, just flour it a little then bring it together in your hands.

Roll it out to 3mm (⅛in) thick between 2 pieces of baking parchment, lightly floured if necessary. Depending on what size tartlet tins (pans) you are using, cut the pastry to fit the tins (pans) and line them. I use 6cm (2½in) tins (pans), lightly buttered, and a 6cm (2½in) biscuit (cookie) cutter. These make a few good mouthfuls so, for canapés, you might like to use slightly smaller tins (pans). Rest the lined tins (pans) in the fridge for 30 minutes while you prepare the fillings. They can also be frozen at this point for up to 1 month, either as tart shells, or as a piece of pastry before you roll it out.

Preheat the oven to 180°C/350°F/gas mark 4. Bake the rye pastry shells for 10–12 minutes, until a little darkened and hard to the touch. Leave to cool in the tins (pans) on a wire rack before removing from the tins (pans) and filling.

Store any leftover pastry shells in an airtight container in a cool place for up to 5 days.

Roast garlic, shallot, leek and gorgonzola pasties with thyme, rosemary and parsley pastry

The addition of crème fraîche makes for a deliciously light and flaky pastry (pie crust), packed with flavour from the nutty wholegrain spelt flour, with the herbs adding their oomph and really complementing the filling. I love their hints of green through the pastry, too. This is a filling but not heavy pasty, great for a winter lunch, or at the end of the day, served with soup and a salad.

MAKES 9–10

For the filling
1 garlic bulb
200g (7oz) banana shallots (about 6 small shallots), unpeeled weight
sea salt flakes and freshly ground black pepper
4 tbsp extra virgin olive oil, plus more for the garlic and shallots
2 large leeks, about 400g (14oz) total weight
150g (5½oz) *gorgonzola dolce* cheese

For the pastry (pie dough)
250g (9oz / generous 2 cups) wholegrain spelt flour
100g (3½oz / scant 1 cup) white spelt flour, plus more to dust
5 tbsp finely chopped parsley leaves
1 tbsp finely chopped rosemary needles
1 tbsp finely chopped thyme leaves
225g (8oz / 1 cup / 2 sticks) cold unsalted butter, cut into 1cm (½in) cubes
125g (4½oz / ½ cup) crème fraîche

Preheat the oven to 200°C/400°F/gas mark 6. Remove the cloves from the garlic bulb and place them, skins on, on a small baking tray (sheet). Cut off the ends of the shallots, peel them and cut each into 3. Add them to the garlic cloves with a generous pinch of salt, pepper and a good glug of olive oil and roast for 15–20 minutes, or until caramel brown and soft.

Meanwhile, trim off just the tops of the leeks and their roots, finely slice them and give them a good wash. Put a saucepan over a medium heat with the 4 tbsp of olive oil. Add the leeks, salt and pepper, stir and then cover with a lid to sweat them down until very soft. Set aside.

Make the pastry by mixing together the flours, 1 tsp salt, a pinch of pepper and the chopped herbs. Disperse the ingredients with a whisk. Using a freestanding mixer fitted with a paddle, add the butter cubes and mix until crumbs form. Add the crème fraîche and mix until just combined. Bring the mix together in your hands to form a ball; the pastry may seem a bit wet, but that's fine. If it's very soft and warm, wrap it in cling film (plastic wrap) and chill for about 15 minutes before continuing. If you have worked quickly with cold butter and the pastry is cool, carry on with the rolling now.

Roll out the pastry between 2 pieces of baking parchment, lightly flouring the bottom piece and the top of the pastry, until no thicker than a £1 coin. Cut out 12.5cm (5in) discs, place on 2 baking trays (sheets) lined with baking parchment, and chill for 30 minutes, or until you have made the filling.

Remove the garlic and shallots from the oven. Reduce the oven temperature to 180°C/350°F/gas mark 4. Squeeze out the garlic flesh into the leeks, then add the shallots, slicing up any larger pieces. Roughly chop the gorgonzola (keep some larger pieces), tumble it in and stir once. Taste for seasoning.

Fill half of each pastry disc with some of the filling, dividing the mix between the shells and squeezing it a little to compact it, leaving a 2cm (¾in) edge. Fold other half over and crimp to seal. You might have about 1 tbsp of filling left. Cut a cross in the top of each pasty. Bake for 20 minutes, or until golden brown. Eat warm from the oven, or they're great cold, too, and will keep for about 5 days in the fridge. The pastry can also be frozen for up to 1 month.

Variation: Ham or bacon pieces make a yummy addition to the filling.

Pumpkin, spinach and ricotta pie with oregano and pine nuts

During my modern languages degree, I spent five months in Bologna in the north of Italy, also known as *Bologna La Grassa* for all its rich and divine food. The fresh pasta I tasted there will never be forgotten. Two of my favourites were *tortelli di zucca* and *tortelli con ricotta e Parmigiano*, plump parcels filled with pumpkin, and ricotta and Parmesan, served with lots of olive oil or butter and extra cheese. I've combined these fillings here and added oregano, a wonderful herb that is slightly less pungent than sage. The filling is encased in crunchy filo (phyllo) and, once the vegetables are cooked, it's quick and easy to make.

Squash will work instead of pumpkin, but find the most flavoursome type, as some can be quite watery.

SERVES 4–6

1 pumpkin, about 850g (1lb 14oz), peeled, cored and cut into cubes (see recipe introduction)
2 garlic cloves, finely chopped
sea salt flakes and freshly ground black pepper
110g (3¾oz / scant ½ cup) extra virgin olive oil, plus about 60g (2oz / ¼ cup) for the filo (phyllo) pastry, plus more if needed and for the tin (pan)
300g (10½oz / 10 cups) spinach leaves
250g (9oz / generous 1 cup) ricotta cheese
80g (2¾oz) Parmesan cheese, grated
3 tbsp finely chopped oregano leaves, plus more to serve (optional)
7 sheets of filo (phyllo) pastry (my sheets were 48 x 25.5cm / 19 x 10in)
100g (3½oz / scant ½ cup) mascarpone cheese
30g (1oz / ¼ cup) pine nuts

Preheat the oven to 200°C/400°F/gas mark 6. Roast the pumpkin for about 30 minutes with the garlic, salt and pepper and 40g (1½oz / scant ¼ cup) of the olive oil, until very soft and becoming golden at the edges.

Bring a saucepan of lightly salted water to the boil, then drop the spinach in to cook for 1 minute, no more. Plunge into a bowl of cold water, then drain through a colander, squeezing out all the excess water. Roughly chop.

In a bowl, mash the cooked pumpkin and all its cooking juices with a fork. Mash in the chopped spinach, ricotta, 70g (2½oz / generous ¼ cup) of the olive oil, the Parmesan, oregano and salt and pepper. Taste and adjust the seasoning if necessary; add more olive oil, too, if it seems dry. You want to create a flavoursome, juicy filling that will not become dry when cooked.

Reduce the oven temperature to 180°C/350°F/gas mark 4 and brush a 30 x 20 x 3cm (12 x 8 x 1¼in) or similar sized baking tin (pan) or ovenproof dish with olive oil. Add 1 layer of pastry, brush generously with olive oil, then add another layer of pastry and oil, continuing until you have used all 7 sheets. An even distribution of the filo (phyllo) is necessary, so place 1 sheet horizontally, then 2 sheets lengthways, and so on. Brush the last sheet with oil, then spread over the pumpkin and ricotta mix.

Using a spoon, evenly distribute spoonfuls of the mascarpone over the top of the tart, then swirl it into the pumpkin mix with a fork. Scatter over the pine nuts. Lift up the edges of the filo (phyllo) pastry, tuck them into the sides and corners of the tray and brush them with olive oil. Bake in the oven for 20 minutes, until the edges are golden brown. To serve, drizzle with olive oil, sprinkle with a little salt and add the extra oregano leaves, if you want.

Serve warm or slightly cooled, but it's best eaten fresh. Store any leftovers in the fridge for about 5 days, warming up a little before serving, if you like.

Variation: I also love to make canapés with this mix, layering up filo (phyllo) pastry squares in tartlet tins (pans) and adding the filling (see page 151).

Chicken, chard and tarragon pie

I just adore tarragon and how the herb's bittersweet and subtle anise notes sink into the chicken in this recipe. Mixed with succulent chard stems and their leaves, crème fraîche, the chicken's roasting juices and finely chopped lemon zest, it's a completely joyous filling, encased in the most wonderful nutty, rich emmer pastry. Emmer, an ancient durum wheat known as farro in Italy, was one of the first grains cultivated by man. Its earthy, subtly sweet flavour and creamy texture work so well here in the pastry and with the filling.

Serves 12–16

For the filling
1 medium chicken, about 1.4kg
   (3lb 2½oz)
½ lemon, halved
1 small onion, quartered, skin left on
3 garlic cloves, crushed, skins left on
extra virgin olive oil
sea salt flakes and freshly ground
   black pepper
600g (1lb 5oz) chard leaves and stems
350g (12oz / 1½ cups) crème fraîche
large bunch of tarragon (50g / 1¾oz),
   leaves stripped and roughly chopped

For the pastry (pie dough)
225g (8oz / 1 cup / 2 sticks) cold
   unsalted butter, cut into cubes,
   plus more for the tin (pan)
450g (1lb / scant 3½ cups) wholegrain
   emmer flour, plus more to dust
1½ tsp sea salt flakes
4 medium eggs, plus 1 egg yolk to glaze
1 tbsp whole milk

Preheat the oven to 200°C/400°F/gas mark 6. Place the chicken in a roasting tin (pan) and stuff the cavity with the lemon, onion and garlic. Drizzle the skin with olive oil and season with salt and pepper. Roast for 1 hour, or until the juices run clear when it is pierced through the thick part of a thigh.

Butter a 23cm (9in) springform cake tin (pan). Line with baking parchment. Make the pastry. In a freestanding mixer fitted with a paddle, combine the flour and salt. Add the cubes of butter and mix until it resembles crumbs. Mix the eggs with a fork and add, mixing to combine. (The pastry can be frozen at this point for up to 1 month.) Place two-thirds of the dough (about 610g / 1lb 5oz) on a lightly floured piece of baking parchment. Cover with more flour, then another piece of parchment and roll out into a 3mm- (⅛in-) thick circle big enough to line the prepared tin (pan), then line the tin (pan). Trim the edges and chill for 30 minutes. Roll out the second piece into a rough circle about 25cm (10in) in diameter and chill between the 2 pieces of parchment.

Preheat the oven to 180°C/350°F/gas mark 4. Line the pastry shell with baking parchment and fill with baking beans. Blind bake for 15 minutes. Remove the beans and paper and bake for a further 10 minutes, or until golden brown and hard to the touch.

Meanwhile, heat a saucepan with hot water and salt it a little. Remove the chard leaves from the stems, then cut the stems into rough 1cm (½in) pieces. Place the stems in the boiling water with the leaves on top; boil for 1 minute. Strain through a colander and, when cool, squeeze out the chard leaves.

Remove the meat from the chicken; you want 500g (1lb 2oz) of meat. Rip into large bite-sized pieces and place in a bowl. Squeeze any of the juice from the lemon over, then chop up the peel finely and add that, too. Add 100g (3½oz / generous ⅓ cup) of the chicken's cooking juices, the crème fraîche, tarragon leaves and chard, ripping up the chard leaves as they are added. Mix and season well. Put in the baked tart shell. Mix the egg yolk with the milk and brush this over the rim. Take out the chilled circle of pastry and flip it on to the top, pressing it into the edges to stick, folding over excess and crimping it. Brush the top with the remaining yolk mix. Cut a cross in the middle and bake for 30 minutes, or until golden brown and firm to the touch.

Leave to cool slightly in the tin (pan), then enjoy warm. Keep any leftovers in a sealed container in the fridge for about 4 days.

Asparagus, prosciutto, Taleggio and marjoram quiche with walnut pastry

It's great to have a reliable quiche recipe in your repertoire. This pastry (pie dough) is perfectly crumbly with a crunch from the nuts, the white flour keeping it light while wholegrain flour adds a good depth of flavour. The filling is unctuous and delectable with the creamy Taleggio. If this mix is not for you, or asparagus is not in season, play around with whatever you like, using the base recipes for the pastry shell and quiche filling.

Serves 10–12

For the pastry (pie dough)
150g (5½oz / ⅔ cup / 1¼ sticks) cold unsalted butter, cut into cubes, plus more for the tin (pan)

75g (2¾oz / ¾ cup) walnuts

115g (4oz / scant 1 cup) white wheat flour, plus more to dust

115g (4oz / scant 1 cup) wholegrain wheat flour

1 tsp sea salt flakes

1 egg, plus 1 egg yolk, plus 1 egg yolk for the glaze

For the filling
sea salt flakes and freshly ground black pepper

400g (14oz) asparagus, ends snapped off

15g (½oz / 1 tbsp) wholegrain or white wheat flour

165g (5¾oz / generous ⅔ cup) whole milk

165g (5¾oz / generous ⅔ cup) double (heavy) cream

165g (5¾oz) eggs, about 3 large

160g (5¾oz) Taleggio cheese (weight without skin), in chunks

90g (3¼oz) prosciutto, ripped

5 tbsp marjoram leaves, roughly chopped

Butter a 28cm (11in) loose-bottomed tart tin (pan). In a food processor, roughly chop the walnuts to a bit smaller than pea-sized. In a freestanding mixer fitted with a paddle, combine the nuts, flours and salt. While mixing, add the butter until it resembles crumbs. Mix together the egg and 1 egg yolk and add, mixing until it comes together. Press into a circle. At this point, if the pastry is warm and sticky, wrap it in cling film (plastic wrap) and chill for 30 minutes. If it's still cool, continue straight away.

Roll the pastry between 2 pieces of lightly floured baking parchment, flouring the bottom piece of parchment and the top of the pastry, until about 3mm (⅛in) thick. Flour the pastry, roll it up around the rolling pin and unroll it over the prepared tin (pan), (or flip the pastry into the tin / pan). Press the pastry into the tin (pan), folding any overlapping edges over to make the rim double the thickness. Rest the pastry shell in the fridge for 30 minutes.

Preheat the oven to 180°C/350°F/gas mark 4. Line the pastry shell with baking parchment and fill with baking beans. Blind bake for 10 minutes. Remove the parchment and baking beans and bake for a further 15–20 minutes, until a good golden brown. Brush the shell with the extra egg yolk, making sure to seal any cracks, and bake for 2 minutes to dry out; repeat this process if there are any more cracks to seal. Remove from the oven.

Bring a saucepan of water to the boil and add a good pinch of salt. Drop in the asparagus and cook for a few minutes until just tender. Drain and run under cold water until cool, then pat dry. Cut into about 3cm (1¼in) pieces. Meanwhile, whisk the quiche filling ingredients from the flour to the eggs, then season well. (I often add a little flour to quiche fillings, to thicken them.)

Fill the quiche shell by alternating between the asparagus, cheese, prosciutto and marjoram. Season with salt and pepper. Place on a tray in the oven, give the liquid filling a mix, then pour it over the quiche filling to just fill the shell. Close the oven door, reduce the oven temperature to 160°C/325°F/gas mark 3 and bake for 30 minutes, until the filling has just set. Leave to cool.

Variation: This milk, cream and egg quiche filling is also delicious baked alone, without the pastry, adding any fillings from spinach to broccoli and mushrooms to other herbs. Bake at 160°C/325°F/gas mark 3 in ramekins, or an ovenproof dish, for about 10 or 20 minutes respectively, or until just set with a little wobble.

Tart of summer greens with buckwheat, oat and hazelnut pastry

Pastry (pie crust) doesn't need to be made with only flour; adding nuts, seeds and oats or other flakes can give so much more texture and interest, while herbs and dried flowers are also great. Try playing around with your pastry recipes and your favourite nuts, grains and flavours. This crunchy open tart base provides a perfect blank canvas for summer vegetables galore, or use it at any time of year with whatever is in season, changing the hazelnuts and oat flakes, too, if you like. It's an eat-with-your-fingers kind of tart that is perfect for picnics. The pastry dough can also be made into delicious savoury biscuits (cookies) to enjoy with things like hummus and cheese.

Serves 10–12

For the pastry (pie dough)
140g (5oz / 1½ cups) rolled oats
140g (5oz / 1 cup) buckwheat flour
2 tsp sea salt flakes
140g (5oz / scant 1 cup) hazelnuts, blanched, or whole with skins
10 tbsp cold water
120g (4¼oz / scant ⅔ cup) virgin coconut oil, melted

For the topping
extra virgin olive oil
1 fennel bulb, outer leaves removed, finely sliced
2 courgettes (zucchini), sliced with a vegetable peeler into ribbons
160g (5¾oz / generous 1 cup) peas, fresh or frozen
140g (5oz) asparagus, or green beans or runner beans, or mangetout (snow peas)
30g (1oz) herb leaves such as parsley, chives or basil, finely chopped
40g (1½oz / 1½ cups) baby spinach leaves, watercress, or rocket (arugula)
freshly ground black pepper
finely grated zest and juice of 1 unwaxed lemon
170g (6oz) soft cheese, such as Brie, goat's cheese or curd, or burrata (optional)
garlic chive flowers and other edible flowers, to decorate (optional)

Preheat the oven to 180°C/350°F/gas mark 4. Line a baking tray (sheet) with baking parchment.

Put the oats, flour and salt in a food processor and blitz a few times to combine. Add the hazelnuts and process until relatively fine, but with some larger pieces for bite. Add the water and coconut oil to the food processor and blend everything once more until it comes together.

Turn the mix out on to the prepared tray (sheet) and pat it out to make a rectangle with rounded corners, about 20cm (8in) wide and 37cm (14½in) long. Bake for about 30 minutes, checking after 20 minutes, or until golden brown and firm to the touch. Leave to cool on the tray (sheet).

Meanwhile, prepare the vegetables. Heat a griddle pan with a few tbsp of extra virgin olive oil. Add the fennel and cook in the griddle pan until marked on each side and a little soft. Place in a large bowl. Repeat the griddling process with the courgettes (zucchini) (or leave the ribbons raw, if you prefer, or griddle some and leave others raw), adding them to the fennel.

Bring a saucepan of water to the boil and add a few pinches of salt. Drop in the peas and cook until tender. Remove with a slotted spoon and plunge into cold water. Repeat the process for the asparagus, beans or mangetout (snow peas). Strain off the water. Slice the asparagus, beans or mangetout (snow peas) on the slant, about 3cm (1¼in) long, then add to the courgettes (zucchini) and fennel with the peas. Add the fresh herbs and leaves, salt, pepper, lemon zest and half the juice and mix up with your hands. Taste for seasoning and adjust as necessary.

Rip up or crumble in the cheese, if using, and lightly toss everything once more, then spread it all out over the cooked tart base and serve with an extra drizzle of extra virgin olive oil and squeeze of lemon juice. I like to add garlic chive flowers and edible flowers such as nasturtiums or marigolds, to decorate.

Tomato, *ricotta salata* and aubergine (eggplant) tarte Tatin with Pecorino pastry

This is such a delicious, robust, cheesy, woody, nutty pastry (pie crust), the exterior remaining flaky-light while the inner part absorbs all the juices from the slightly caramelized aubergines (eggplants) and tomatoes. It's the gluten-free buckwheat flour and cheese that make it so irresistibly crumbly. I like to serve up slices with *ricotta salata*, black olives and basil leaves, reminding me of a divine bowl of pasta alla Norma I ate in Italy years ago. It's great as a starter (appetizer) or main course with a big summery salad.

Serves 4–6

For the pastry (pie dough)
100g (3½oz / ¾ cup) wholegrain wheat flour
50g (1¾oz / ⅓ cup) buckwheat flour, plus more to dust
75g (2¾oz / 1 cup) grated Pecorino cheese
pinch of sea salt flakes
75g (2¾oz / ⅓ cup) cold unsalted butter, cubed
1 egg, lightly beaten

For the filling
6 tbsp extra virgin olive oil, plus more to serve
1 red or white onion, finely sliced
2 garlic cloves, crushed
1 good-sized aubergine (eggplant), finely sliced into 5mm (¼in) slices
sea salt flakes and freshly ground black pepper
3 good-sized tomatoes, cut into 1cm (½in) slices, spread on a board and sprinkled with salt
60g–80g (2–2¾oz) *ricotta salata* cheese, coarsely grated
handful of basil leaves
up to 60g (2oz / generous ½ cup) black olives

Choose an ovenproof frying pan (skillet) about 20cm (8in) in diameter.

Start by making the pastry. Combine the flours, Pecorino and salt in a freestanding mixer fitted with a paddle, or by hand, add the butter and combine until the mix resembles crumbs. Add the egg and mix once more until the pastry comes together. Bring it together in your hands, then pat out on to a piece of lightly floured baking parchment. Flour the top, cover with another piece of baking parchment and roll out into a 20cm (8in) diameter rough circle. Place on a tray and chill in the fridge.

Preheat the oven to 180°C/350°F/gas mark 4.

Heat 2 tbsp olive oil in the frying pan (skillet) and add the sliced onion and garlic. Cook for about 5 minutes, then add the aubergine (eggplant) and 2 more tbsp olive oil. Season well and cook for about 10 minutes, until the aubergine (eggplant) is soft and the onion is golden. Remove from the pan to a plate. Add the final 2 tbsp olive oil and then start to layer in the slices of aubergine (eggplant), tomatoes and onion, overlapping them like petals, starting from the edge and working into the centre until all the ingredients have been used up.

Remove the chilled pastry from the fridge and press it lightly over the vegetables, sealing the edges.

Bake for 20 minutes, or until the pastry is golden brown. Remove from the oven and, after about 5 minutes, slide a knife around the edge, put a serving plate over the pastry, then flip it over on to the plate using oven gloves.

Drizzle the tart with olive oil and serve slices with *ricotta salata*, basil leaves and black olives.

Store any leftovers in the fridge for up to 5 days. The pastry can be wrapped in cling film (plastic wrap) and stored in the freezer for at least 1 month.

Note: This pastry is very versatile and, grated over cooked vegetables, is great as a savoury crumble topping.

Grilled spinach gnocchi with Fontal, mascarpone and mushroom

I'll never forget eating fresh gnocchi cooked by my friend's Italian mother. Soft, light and a complete joy. It took me a while to make them myself, as I thought they would be terribly difficult... but they're not, and it's immensely satisfying both to make and, finally, taste them in their pillow-soft glory. Though they're wonderful without any additions, these are enriched with spinach and nutmeg, then grilled (broiled) with a sublime mushroom sauce topped with Fontal, a lovely cheese a little bit like Fontina but less earthy and more creamy, so it does not overpower the other flavours. Perfect with a green salad.

SERVES ABOUT 4

For the gnocchi

500g (1lb 2oz) potatoes (I use
  Maris Piper)
115g (4oz / generous ¾ cup) 00 flour,
  plus more to dust
1 medium egg, lightly beaten
25g (1oz / 2 tbsp) unsalted butter,
  softened
100g (3½oz / generous 3 cups) spinach,
  blanched, drained, water squeezed out
  and chopped (see page 114)
¼ nutmeg, grated
sea salt flakes and freshly ground
  black pepper
extra virgin olive oil
10 sage leaves

For the sauce

3 generous tbsp extra virgin olive oil,
  plus more to serve
2 garlic cloves, finely chopped
1 banana shallot (about 60g/2oz),
  finely chopped
250g (9oz / 3½ cups) chestnut (cremini)
  mushrooms, sliced about 2mm
  (⅛in) thick
250g (9oz / generous 1 cup)
  mascarpone cheese
5 tbsp white wine
1 tbsp thyme leaves, plus more to serve
250g (9oz) Fontal cheese (weight without
  skin), sliced about 3mm (⅛in) thick

Cover the potatoes with water in a large saucepan, bring to the boil and cook until soft. Drain, cool slightly and remove the skins. When they are still warm, mash them through a relatively fine sieve into a bowl. Add the flour, egg and butter and mix with your hands to combine. Add the cooked chopped spinach, a good grating of nutmeg and salt and mix once more.

Meanwhile, make the sauce. In a saucepan, heat the olive oil. Add the garlic and shallot and cook until soft and becoming golden. Add the mushrooms, continuing to cook until soft. Add the mascarpone, white wine and salt and pepper to taste. When it's all bubbling and looking creamy, remove from the heat and stir in the thyme leaves. Set aside.

Preheat the grill (broiler). Place a large pan filled with slightly salted water over a medium-high heat and bring to the boil.

On a lightly floured surface, divide the mixture into 2, rolling each into a cylinder 2cm (¾in) in diameter. Cut each cylinder at 1.5cm (¾in) intervals.

Once the water is boiling, drop in half the gnocchi and cook for 2–3 minutes, or until they float to the surface. Remove with a spider (a mesh ladle) or slotted spoon and place on kitchen paper or a tea towel to absorb excess water. Repeat for the remaining gnocchi.

Place an ovenproof pan large enough to fit all the gnocchi over a medium heat and add a few tbsp of olive oil. Rip up the sage leaves, add them to the pan and cook for 1 minute. Reduce the heat to low, add the gnocchi and move them carefully with a wooden spoon to re-warm them. Top with the mushroom sauce and Fontal, then place under the grill (broiler) for 10 minutes, until the sauce is bubbling and the cheese is golden brown. Serve warm, drizzled with extra virgin olive oil and sprinkled with thyme leaves.

Keep any leftovers in the fridge for up to 4 days and warm them through, if you want, before serving.

Brown rice pasta cheese with rye crumbs

This is just like a macaroni cheese but with lots of tasty alternatives and extras. Instead of traditional macaroni, I've used brown rice pasta, which has a great texture very similar to that of regular pasta, and a subtly robust flavour that works really well with the nuttiness of the rye, mature (sharp) Cheddar and earthy, rich pockets of Brie, while thyme leaves just lift it all up. The slight sourness of the rye crumb – especially if you use a sourdough rye – is gorgeous with the creamy cheese sauce. A filling and scrumptious end to the day, and rather good cold or warmed up for lunch the next day, too!

If you're using greens that take longer to cook, such as broccoli or broad beans (fava beans), cook them before adding to the mixture.

SERVES 2–4

150g (5½oz / 2 cups) brown rice pasta
50g (1¾oz / 3½ tbsp) unsalted butter
5 tbsp rye flour
250g (9oz / generous 1 cup) whole milk
90g (3¼oz) mature (sharp) Cheddar
  cheese, coarsely grated
sea salt flakes and freshly ground
  black pepper
½–1 tsp English mustard, or to taste
80g (2¾oz / scant 3 cups) greens, such
  as finely chopped chard, baby spinach
  leaves or fresh peas
1 generous tsp thyme leaves, plus more
  to serve
60g (2oz) bacon lardons, cooked until
  golden brown (optional)
60g (2oz) Brie cheese, roughly chopped
  into 2cm (¾in) chunks
nutmeg, grated
100g (3½oz / 2 cups) rye breadcrumbs,
  preferably sourdough

Preheat the oven to 180°C/350°F/gas mark 4. Cook the pasta, following the instructions on the packet (but starting to check before the end of the suggested cooking time), until al dente. Drain and reserve the cooking water.

Make a roux by melting the butter in a saucepan. Add the rye flour and quickly stir in with a wooden spoon. Gradually add the milk, whisking it in until the mix is just boiling around the edges and thick and creamy. Add the Cheddar, salt, pepper and mustard and taste for seasoning, adding more salt, pepper and mustard if necessary. Add the pasta, greens, thyme and bacon, if using, and stir together. If the mix looks stiff, add some of the leftover pasta cooking water.

Pour into a suitable ovenproof dish, I use a 20cm (8in) pot or a 24cm (9½in) oval dish. Push the pieces of Brie slightly into the pasta. Grate a little nutmeg over the top, sprinkle with the breadcrumbs and a little salt and pepper and cook for 15 minutes, or until bubbling. The top should be golden brown and looking crunchy. Serve with extra thyme and steamed green vegetables, or a salad.

Mozzarella, Parmesan and polenta (cornmeal) pot

Before a friend cooked me a wonderfully simple and delicious meal of creamy, unctuous polenta (cornmeal) with roast vegetables and sausages, I'd only really used it in cakes. But it's such a useful, versatile ingredient and so easy to use in savoury dishes, too, plus it makes a lovely alternative to pasta. Here, I bake it until it's firm, then colourful roast vegetables are added, all their tasty cooking juices seeping into the polenta, and it's returned to the oven with a layer of mozzarella, creating a light but filling and rich summer dish.

SERVES 4–6

1 red (bell) pepper
1 orange (bell) pepper
1 yellow (bell) pepper
2 onions, finely sliced
3 garlic cloves, crushed or finely chopped
350g–400g (12–14oz) courgettes (zucchini) (about 4 medium), cut into generous 1cm (½in) circles
100g (3½oz / generous ⅓ cup) extra virgin olive oil, plus 3 tbsp, plus more for the dish and if needed
sea salt flakes and freshly ground black pepper
500g (1lb 2oz / 2 cups) water
50g (1¾oz) Parmesan cheese, grated, plus more to serve
1 generous tbsp chopped oregano leaves, plus more to serve (optional)
1 tbsp thyme leaves, plus more to serve (optional)
2 generous tbsp chopped basil leaves, plus more to serve (optional)
100g (3½oz / ⅔ cup) quick cook polenta (cornmeal)
2 branches of vine tomatoes, about 200g (7oz) total weight
250g (9oz) mozzarella
basil oil, to serve (optional)
a little finely grated unwaxed lemon zest

Preheat the oven to 200°C/400°F/gas mark 6.

Slice the peppers into rough 2cm (¾in) strips. Place them, along with the onions, garlic, courgettes (zucchini) and extra virgin olive oil, in a roasting tray. Season well with salt and pepper, mix together and roast for 45 minutes to 1 hour or until all the vegetables are soft, golden brown and caramelizing. Set aside.

Reduce the oven temperature to 180°C/350°F/gas mark 4.

Oil an ovenproof round dish, about 22cm (8½in) in diameter and 5cm (2in) deep. Bring the water to the boil in a saucepan and add the Parmesan and herbs. Then add the polenta (cornmeal) and whisk continuously over a medium heat until thick and creamy. This will take about 10 minutes. Remove from the heat, add 2 tbsp extra virgin olive oil and season to taste. Pour into the prepared dish and bake for 10 minutes, or until just firm to touch. At the same time, remove the tomatoes from the vine, place on a baking tray (sheet) with the remaining 1 tbsp extra virgin olive oil, salt and pepper and bake for 5–10 minutes, until the skins start to come off and the tomatoes are softening.

Increase the oven temperature to 200°C/400°F/gas mark 6 once more.

Place the roast pepper mixture over the baked polenta (cornmeal), along with all its juices. Arrange the tomatoes evenly over that and pour over their juices, too. Rip the mozzarella over everything. Bake for 10 minutes, or until the mozzarella is melting and just becoming golden. If you like, drizzle with a little extra olive oil, or basil oil, if you have it.

Finish with a little lemon zest, extra chopped herbs and Parmesan shavings, if you want. Serve warm from the oven, in warmed bowls, with a green salad.

Store any leftovers in the fridge for up to 4 days, warming a little in the oven before serving, if you like. By this stage, the polenta (cornmeal) will have hardened, but it's still just as tasty.

Wild garlic, dandelion and goat's cheese *gözleme*

Spring is one of the most wonderful times of year. After the barren winter months, suddenly trees are covered in green leaves, white and pink blossom is all around and spring greens are coming along. While I pass a wonderful café making fresh *gözleme* (filled Turkish flatbreads) every day near my house in London, I return to the country in the spring and find wild garlic, nestled among bluebells in the woods, and dandelions. Biting into these, you get a hit of punchy wild garlic, a little bitterness from the dandelion, then the creamy goat's cheese, all encased in a soft and nutty wholegrain dough… Just delicious!

Makes 5

For the dough

200g (7oz / scant 1½ cups) strong
    wholegrain wheat flour
100g (3½oz / ¾ cup) strong white wheat
    flour, plus more to dust
½ tsp dried yeast
1 tsp sea salt flakes
100g (3½oz / generous ⅓ cup) natural
    yogurt
200g (7oz / generous ¾ cup) lukewarm
    water
extra virgin olive oil

For the filling

130g (4¾oz) wild garlic leaves, washed
    and finely chopped
130g (4¾oz) dandelion leaves, the
    younger and smaller the better,
    washed and finely chopped
300g (10½oz) soft goat's cheese,
    crumbled
50g (1¾oz) wild garlic flowers, washed
8–10 tbsp extra virgin olive oil, plus
    more to cook
finely grated zest of 1 unwaxed lemon
sea salt flakes and freshly ground
    black pepper

In a bowl, mix together the flours, yeast and salt using a whisk. Add the yogurt and water, mix with a wooden spoon. Cover with a tea towel and leave to stand for 15 minutes. Knead for 1 minute until smooth, adding more flour if necessary so the dough is not too sticky. Shape into a ball and place in an oiled bowl. Cover with a tea towel and leave for 1 hour in a warm place.

Divide into 5 balls, each should weigh 110–120g (3¼–4¼oz). Flour a work surface well, place a ball of dough on top, flour it, then roll it into a thin, 25cm (10in) diameter circle, making sure to keep lifting it from the work surface so it does not stick. If it is very sticky, just use more flour.

Mix together the chopped wild garlic and dandelion leaves. For each *gözleme*, spread 50g (1¾oz) of the greens out on to the centre of the rolled out dough, leaving about 7.5cm (3in) of dough uncovered at the bottom and top and 5cm (2in) on each side. Top with 60g (2oz) goat's cheese, a scattering of wild garlic flowers, a good tbsp of olive oil and some lemon zest, and season with salt and pepper. Flip over the edges and then the top and bottom, sealing them together like an envelope. Lightly flour the filled dough and work surface and roll out the *gözleme* to flatten and seal it.

Heat an oiled frying pan (skillet) over a heavy-based, flat (not ridged) griddle pan over a high heat. Fry each *gözleme* for 2–3 minutes on each side until golden brown. Eat immediately, or keep on a plate in a warm oven while you quickly cook the rest. Enjoy with a salad, if you like.

Variation: When wild garlic is out of season, or not readily available, try using the same weight of other flavoursome greens and herbs. When I made these for the photo in late August, I used a mixture of chard and rocket (arugula), beetroot (beet) leaves, chives, basil and parsley, and sprinkled the greens with garlic chive flowers. There are many possible fillings as the seasons change, so try to find your favourite. Cooked peppers and onions are delicious, while meat such as cooked bacon, minced (ground) meat or chicken, will make a more filling gözleme.

Turmeric, cumin and coriander *pudlas* with baked chilli paneer and fresh mango and ginger chutney

Pudlas, a type of Gujarati pancake, are made with chickpea (garbanzo bean) flour, yogurt and water. They're easy to make and a great vehicle for lots of delicious fillings, so feel free to try others, such as meat or fish, if you prefer. I worked on this recipe with my good friend and expert in Indian cookery, Meera Sodha, as I've always loved paneer but never knew how to prepare and cook it; as I found out, it's actually very simple! It's often fried, but here we baked it, for a pillow-soft interior, encompassed in a garlic, chilli and cumin sauce, which gets a crust as it bakes. The quick chutney, a spoonful of yogurt and lots of fresh coriander (cilantro) lifts everything up. It's a wonderful, light but filling, flavoursome meal. Thank you, Meera.

SERVES 6

For the paneer
8 tbsp natural yogurt
4 tbsp chickpea (garbanzo bean) flour
6 garlic cloves, finely chopped or grated
4 tbsp tomato purée (paste)
2 tsp chilli powder
1½ tsp sea salt flakes
3 tsp cumin seeds, coarsely crushed
450g (1lb) paneer, in 2cm (¾in) cubes

For the chutney
1 semi-ripe mango, sliced into fine strips
juice of ½ lime, plus lime wedges to serve
10g (¼oz) peeled fresh root ginger, finely chopped
½ tsp sea salt flakes
1 tsp light brown muscovado or coconut sugar, or to taste
1 green finger chilli, finely chopped
freshly ground black pepper

For the *pudlas*
100g (3½oz / ¾ cup) chickpea (garbanzo bean) flour
50g (1¾oz / scant ¼ cup) natural yogurt, plus more to serve
170g (6oz / ¾ cup) cool water, or as needed
¼ tsp baking powder
½ tsp sea salt flakes
1 tbsp chopped coriander (cilantro) leaves, plus leaves from 1 large bunch of coriander (cilantro), to serve
½ tsp cumin seeds, coarsely crushed
¾ tsp ground turmeric
extra virgin cold-pressed rapeseed (canola) oil, to cook

Start by marinating the paneer. Mix all the ingredients together from the yogurt to the cumin seeds. Check for seasoning. Add the cubes of paneer and stir until they are all coated with the sauce. Leave in a cool place while you make the chutney.

Mix together all the chutney ingredients and taste for seasoning, adding more salt, pepper and sugar if necessary.

Preheat the oven to 200°C/400°F/gas mark 6.

Thread the cubes of paneer on to skewers and put on a baking tray (sheet), trying to prop them up on the sides so they do not touch the bottom of the tray (sheet). Bake for 20–30 minutes, until the marinade is getting a bit of colour and the paneer is soft to the touch.

Meanwhile, make the *pudlas* by mixing together all the ingredients with a whisk. The batter should have the consistency of double (heavy) cream, so add a bit more water if necessary. Heat a large non-stick frying pan (skillet) with a little rapeseed (canola) oil, wiping off any excess with kitchen paper. Cook the *pudlas* as if they were pancakes, making sure that there is no runny liquid on the surface before flipping. If the pan is not hot enough, they will stick, so make sure the heat is medium-high. You should get 6 medium-sized *pudlas*. Set each aside on a warmed plate while you quickly cook the rest.

Fill the *pudlas* up with the paneer, sliding it off the skewers, the mango chutney, fresh coriander (cilantro), a squeeze of lime and a spoonful of yogurt.

Variation: Pudlas *are great vehicles for many flavours, so do try them with meat or fish if you prefer, or any Indian-inspired filling.*

Millet, sweet potato and kale cakes with sunflower seed crust

Millet is a very distinctive grain, like no other I know. A bit like quinoa in form, but with a very different flavour which is softer, creamier and subtler than the slight grassiness of quinoa. Cooked millet grain is great in salads and I love it in these cakes, adding a bit of bite to the softness of the sweet potato. Ground sunflower seeds with millet flakes toast up to create a crunchy outer layer, while the thyme combines perfectly with the sweet potatoes and creamy millet. Great for a weekday supper served with fish or chicken, or with a salad and crumbles of feta cheese. Enjoy leftovers for lunch the next day, or even for breakfast with eggs and avocado.

MAKES 8

100g (3½oz / 3 cups) kale leaves, coarse stalks removed (weighed without stalks)
sea salt flakes and freshly ground black pepper
400g (14oz) sweet potatoes (about 2), scrubbed and cubed
120g (4¼oz / ⅔ cup) millet grains
40g (1½oz / ¼ cup) sunflower seeds
40g (1½oz / ⅓ cup) millet flakes
4 tbsp extra virgin olive oil, plus more to drizzle
1 medium red onion, finely chopped
1 large garlic clove, crushed or finely chopped
1 tsp thyme leaves, finely chopped

Cook the kale leaves in boiling salted water for 1 minute, then remove, drain and cool. Squeeze out the water, then chop the leaves.

Preheat the oven to 200°C/400°F/gas mark 6. On a baking tray (sheet) lined with baking parchment, bake the cubed sweet potato for about 30 minutes, or until soft. Place the millet grains in a pan of boiling water to cover and boil for about 10 minutes, until al dente. Strain and rinse with cold water.

Blitz the sunflower seeds and millet flakes with a pinch of salt and pepper in a food processor to form a breadcrumb-like mix. Spread out on a plate and set aside.

Heat 1 tbsp extra virgin olive oil in a small saucepan. Add the red onion and garlic and cook until soft and golden. Remove from the heat and stir in the thyme.

Put the cooked sweet potato pieces, remaining 3 tbsp extra virgin olive oil, red onion and garlic mix and kale in a food processor and process to form a rough paste. Add the cooked millet and process once more to combine. Spoon the mix into a bowl and season to taste. Divide into 8 cakes and pat each side and the edges in the sunflower seed and millet flake mix. Place on a baking tray (sheet) lined with baking parchment, then sprinkle over any remaining coating left on the plate.

Reduce the oven temperature to 180°C/350°F/gas mark 4. Bake the cakes for 10–15 minutes, until they're just getting a bit of colour. Eat with a salad.

Store any leftovers in the fridge for up to 4 days and reheat before serving, if you like.

CHAPTER 5
DESSERTS & PUDDINGS

Fresh fruits are the stars here, dictating which core and magic ingredients will bring out their flavours most delectably.

To cherries I add chocolate and pistachios in a clafoutis; fragrant quince gets a brown sugar meringue, sweet pecans and a Marsala cream; an orange blossom custard is honeyed to lift its flowery notes; while ground almonds help lavender to sing in a pastry with apricots and raspberries. Pastry (pie dough) becomes so much more than just flour, sugar, butter and egg: oats add texture, lavender a floral note, cocoa its richness.

Highlighting the endless flexibility of natural ingredients and how we can use them, this chapter is one of celebration. Core and magic ingredients come together, culminating in the most divine way, as they should, in the final mouthfuls of your meal.

Apricot and raspberry crostata with lavender pastry

A proper crostata – with its pretty lattice top, oozing with fresh fruits encased in crumbly pastry (pie crust) – is a joy. Apricots are one of my favourite fruits and their plump, sweet flesh is delicious with the slightly sharper raspberries, not to mention their vibrant colours. Both fruits work very well with the subtle, fragrant lavender in the pastry (pie dough), which I have made with light white spelt flour, ground almonds and golden caster (superfine) sugar, to allow all the delicate fruity and floral flavours to really sing. I like the lavender to be noticeable but not too strong. If you want a more subtle flavour, use 2 tsp.

Serves 8–10

For the pastry (pie dough)
190g (6¾oz / ¾ cup / 1½ sticks) unsalted butter, cold and cut into cubes, plus more for the tin (pan)
250g (9oz / 2¼ cups) white spelt flour, plus more to dust
50g (1¾oz / ½ cup) ground almonds
½ tsp sea salt flakes
70g (2½oz / ⅓ cup) golden caster (superfine) sugar
2½ tsp dried lavender, roughly chopped
finely grated zest of ½ unwaxed lemon
1 egg, plus 1 egg yolk to seal the pastry

For the filling
8–10 apricots, ripe but still quite firm, (about 400g/14oz in total), pitted and cut into 1cm (½in) slices
finely grated zest of ½ unwaxed lemon
300g (10½oz / 1 cup) apricot jam
300g (10½oz / 2½ cups) raspberries

Butter the sides and base of a 23cm (9in) loose-bottomed tart tin (pan).

Make the pastry by mixing together the flour, almonds, salt, sugar, lavender and lemon zest in a freestanding mixer. Add the cubes of butter and combine until the mixture resembles crumbs. Add the egg and mix once more until it just comes together. Bring the pastry together in your hands and weigh out 300g (10½oz) for the base. Set aside the remaining pastry for the lattice, covering it in cling film (plastic wrap) and resting in the fridge.

Roll the base pastry out to 3mm (⅛in) thick between 2 pieces of baking parchment, lightly flouring the bottom layer of parchment and the top of the pastry, to fit the tin (pan). Lift off the top piece of parchment, roll the pastry around the rolling pin, then unroll it over the tin (pan), pushing it into the edges and trimming off excess. Chill in the fridge for 30 minutes. Roll out the remaining pastry between 2 pieces of baking parchment into a circle a bit more than 3mm (⅛in) thick and return to the fridge on a tray (sheet).

Preheat the oven to 180°C/350°F/gas mark 4. Line the pastry shell with baking parchment and fill with baking beans or raw rice. Blind bake the chilled pastry shell for 10 minutes. Remove the beans or rice and bake the shell for a further 10 minutes, until just golden brown. Brush the baked shell with the extra egg yolk and return to the oven for 1–2 minutes, until just dry. Once cool, combine the apricots, lemon zest and apricot jam in a bowl. Lightly mix in the raspberries, then fill the pastry shell with the fruit mix.

Take the remaining pastry out of the fridge and cut into 1cm- (½in-) wide strips. Make a lattice over the fruit: lie 1 strip lengthways, then 1 horizontal, weaving them through (see photo overleaf), continuing until the top is covered, making sure to press the ends of the lattice into the edge of the pastry shell, that you have brushed with egg yolk, so they stick. Brush the lattice with egg yolk, too. Bake for 30 minutes, until golden brown and bubbling. Leave to cool for 30 minutes, remove from the tin (pan) and serve with cream. Keep any leftovers in the fridge for 5 days. The raw pastry can be frozen for at least 1 month.

Variation: Bake leftover pastry as lavender biscuits (cookies): roll it out to 3mm (⅛in) thick and cut with a 5.5cm (2¼in) fluted cutter. Bake at 180°C/350°F/ gas mark 4 for 8–10 minutes, on a tray (sheet) lined with baking parchment.

Rhubarb and strawberry galette with rose crème pâtissière

The combination of strawberry and rhubarb is one of my favourites, using garden rhubarb rather than forced, that carries on into summer and the strawberry season. It's the fruits' beautiful pink hues and their flavours – at once sharp and sweet – that I adore. With a creamy, fragrant rose custard and the crunch of the spelt crust, there are many textures and flavours in this free-form tart, but they merge brilliantly.

SERVES 10

For the pastry (pie dough)
125g (4½oz / generous 1 cup) wholegrain spelt flour
50g (1¾oz / scant ½ cup) white spelt flour, plus more to dust
pinch of sea salt flakes
finely grated zest of ½ unwaxed lemon
2 tsp light brown muscovado or coconut sugar
115g (4oz / ½ cup / 1 stick) cold unsalted butter, cut into cubes
60g (2oz / ¼ cup) crème fraîche

For the crème pâtissière
250g (9oz / 1 cup) whole milk
¼ vanilla pod (bean), split lengthways, seeds scraped out
3 egg yolks
50g (1¾oz / scant ¼ cup) runny honey
12.5g (¾oz / 2 tsp) cornflour (cornstarch)
1 tsp rose water, or more to taste

For the crumble
20g (¾oz / ¼ cup) ground almonds
20g (¾oz / ¼ cup) whole blanched almonds, or whole almonds with skins
20g (¾oz / 4 tsp) light brown muscovado or coconut sugar

For the filling
300g (10½oz / 2¾ cups) rhubarb, cut into 2cm (¾in) pieces
400g (14oz / 2¾ cups) strawberries, hulled
4 tbsp golden caster (superfine), light brown muscovado or coconut sugar

Start by making the pastry. In the bowl of a freestanding mixer fitted with a paddle, weigh out the flours with the salt, lemon zest and sugar. Process to disperse the ingredients. Add the butter cubes and mix until crumbs form. Add the crème fraîche and mix until just combined. Bring the mix together in your hands to form a ball. Roll into a circle between 2 pieces of baking parchment, flouring the bottom piece and the top of the pastry, as the dough is a little sticky, until 3mm (⅛in) thick and about 28cm (11in) in diameter. Rest in the fridge between the 2 pieces of baking parchment for 30 minutes.

For the crème pâtissière, pour the milk into a saucepan, add the vanilla seeds and pod and bring to the boil. Mix together the egg yolks, honey and cornflour in a bowl, then pour the hot milk over, whisking all the time. Return the mixture to the saucepan and place over a low heat, whisking until thick and just beginning to bubble. Add the rose water, whisk in, taste and add more if you want. Remove from the heat and transfer to a clean bowl to cool, whisking now and again to help the cooling process. When it has cooled a little, press cling film (plastic wrap) directly on to the surface, then chill.

Make the crumble by placing everything in a food processor. Process until fine, but still with some texture from the whole almonds.

Preheat the oven to 180°C/350°F/gas mark 4. Take the pastry out of the fridge and remove the top piece of parchment. Cover it with the crumble, leaving a 4cm (1½in) rim. Spread over the crème pâtissière, then top with the rhubarb and 300g (10½oz / 2 cups) of the strawberries. Carefully roll the edges of the pastry over the filling, pressing them in to keep them secure. Sprinkle the fruit with 2 tbsp of the sugar. Bake for 15 minutes.

Remove from the oven, add the remaining strawberries, filling any gaps, and 1 tbsp more sugar, sprinkling it over the fruit. Bake for 10–15 minutes, or until the edges are golden brown, the cream is bubbling and the rhubarb is soft. Sprinkle with the remaining sugar and serve warm. It's delicious with vanilla ice cream, yogurt or cream.

Keep any leftovers in the fridge for up to 5 days. The raw pastry can be frozen for up to 1 month.

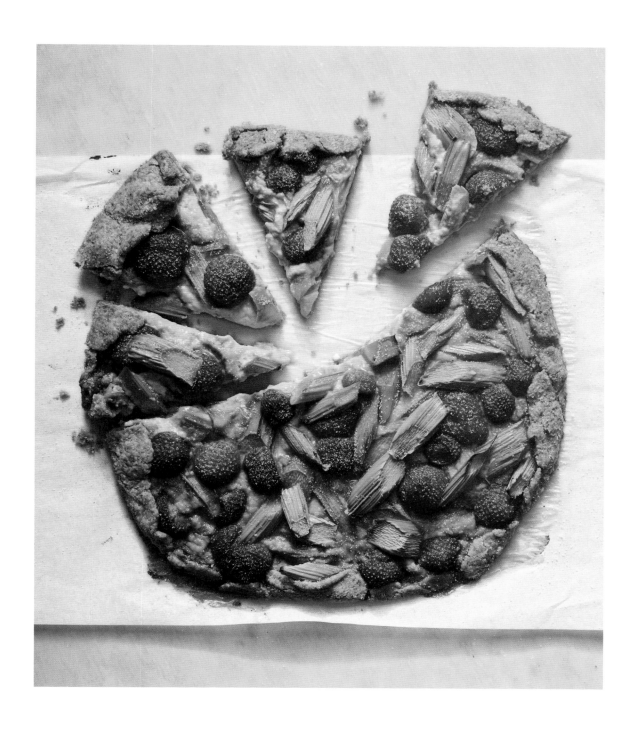

Figgy seeded chocolate water ganache tart with orange and sea salt

Chocolate and orange, or chocolate and sea salt? It's impossibly hard to choose, so I've put them both in together to create this great whip-up-in-moments tart. It makes a sublime dessert served with ice cream or coconut yogurt to wow friends, but also a lovely snack, thanks to the nutrient power-packed seed base.

For the mixed seeds, I like to use two-thirds pumpkin and sunflower seeds and make up the rest of the quantity with sesame, hulled hemp, chia and flaxseeds (linseeds), but just two or three types will be fine. Be aware that chia and flaxseeds (linseeds) are slightly chewier, so stick to crunchier types such as pumpkin, sunflower and sesame, if necessary.

SERVES 12–14

For the base
virgin coconut oil or unsalted butter, for the tin (pan)
300g (10½oz / 2½ cups) dried figs
pinch of sea salt flakes
4 tbsp cocoa or cacao powder
finely grated zest of 1 orange
6 tbsp orange juice
200g (7oz / 1½ cups) mixed seeds (see recipe introduction)

For the ganache
200g (7oz) 85% cocoa solids dark chocolate, chopped
200g (7oz / generous ¾ cup) boiling water
2 tbsp maple syrup
1 tsp vanilla extract
pinch of sea salt flakes, plus more to serve
edible flowers, to serve (optional)

Rub a 24cm (9½in) loose-bottomed tart tin (pan) with coconut oil or butter. Line the base with baking parchment.

For the base, soak the figs in enough warm water to cover for 10 minutes. Strain, cut off the stalks and roughly chop the fruits. Place the figs, salt, cocoa or cacao powder, orange zest and juice in a food processor and blend, scraping down the edges and blending again a few times to form a smooth paste. Add the mixed seeds and process again to combine with the fig paste, stopping the processor and moving the mix with a spoon to help.

Turn the mix out of the food processor into the prepared tin (pan), spreading it over the base with your fingers, pressing it up and into the corners to get 1cm- (½in-) thick sides and base. Even out the base with a step or cranked palette knife, or the back of a spoon. Refrigerate.

Place the chocolate in a heatproof bowl and pour over the boiling water followed by the maple syrup, vanilla and salt. Whisk to form a smooth ganache. Pour it over the seed base and return to the fridge for at least 1 hour, or until set.

To serve, sprinkle with a good amount of sea salt flakes and decorate with edible flowers such as pansies, dianthus or geraniums, if you like. This keeps well in the fridge for at least 5 days and also freezes well for up to 1 month.

Honey and walnut tart with wholegrain oat pastry

My grandmother used to come over most Sundays for lunch and was often on pudding duty, we couldn't wait to see her and the delights she brought each weekend. Apple pies with extra pastry (pie crust) on top in the form of apples with leaves, or heavenly *arroz doce* from her childhood spent in Portugal. Her treacle tart was particularly wonderful, so sweet, but with a good dousing of lemon juice. Here's my take on it, which I hope you would have enjoyed, Granny. We are lucky to have a lot of local honey in Suffolk where my parents live and where I grew up, so I've used that in place of the treacle, as I just adore its flavour. I've made the pastry (pie crust) with wholegrain flour and oats; it has a great texture and rich, deep taste that really complements the walnut-honey filling. The pastry makes the best biscuits (cookies), or, without the egg, crumble (bake those using the directions on pages 139 and 105 respectively).

SERVES 10–12

For the pastry (pie dough)
100g (3½oz / ½ cup / 1 stick) cold unsalted butter, cut into cubes, plus more for the tin (pan)
100g (3½oz / 1 cup) rolled oats
100g (3½oz / ¾ cup) wholegrain wheat flour, plus more to dust
50g (1¾oz / ¼ cup) light brown muscovado or coconut sugar
pinch of sea salt flakes
1 egg, plus 1 egg yolk to glaze

For the filling
600g (1lb 5oz / 1¾ cups) honey
2 tbsp lemon juice
150g (5½oz / 3 cups) sourdough breadcrumbs, brown or white (I prefer brown), preferably a few days old
110g (4oz / generous 1 cup) walnuts, the fresher the better

Butter a 33 x 12.5cm (13 x 5in) rectangular tin (pan) or a 24cm (9½in) round tart tin (pan). Line a baking tray (sheet) with baking parchment.

Start by making the pastry. In a freestanding mixer fitted with a paddle, or by hand, combine the oats, flour, sugar and salt. Add the butter and mix until it resembles crumbs. Add the egg and mix once more until everything comes together. The pastry is a little sticky, but this is normal. Bring it together and then flatten into a 2.5cm- (1in-) thick rectangle on a piece of floured baking parchment. Flour the top of the pastry, place another piece of baking parchment on top, then roll it out to the size of the tin (pan) and 3mm (⅛in) thick. Roll the dough up on to the rolling pin, then out over the buttered tin (pan), or just flip it in from the baking parchment (removing the top parchment layer first). Line the tin (pan), trim the edges and leave to rest in the fridge for 30 minutes.

Preheat the oven to 180°C/350°F/gas mark 4. Warm the honey and lemon juice in a saucepan, mix in the breadcrumbs and set aside. Toast the walnuts on the prepared tray (sheet) in the oven for 4 minutes. Cool and chop.

Line the raw pastry shell with a layer of baking parchment and fill with baking beans. Blind bake for 10 minutes. Remove the beans and bake for a further 10 minutes. Brush the shell with the egg yolk and return to the oven for 1–2 minutes to dry out. Once cool, remove the shell from the tin (pan) and place on a baking tray (sheet). It's best to bake the filled tart out of the tin (pan), otherwise, if any honey leaks, it can be hard to get it out!

Fill the shell with the toasted walnuts, then the honey mix. Bake for 25–30 minutes, or until it looks just set and the top of the tart is darkening. Leave to cool slightly to set, then enjoy with vanilla ice cream or cream. Crème fraîche is also very good, its sharpness cutting through the honey's sweetness.

Keep any leftovers in a sealed container in the fridge for up to 5 days. The raw pastry can be frozen, in cling film (plastic wrap) or in the lined tart tin (pan), for at least 1 month.

Fig and lemon verbena curd toasted oat pastry tartlets with yogurt and honeycomb

The delicate flavours of lemon verbena and figs need this light-tasting pastry (pie crust), to which toasted oats add a subtle but lovely nutty creaminess and another texture, that I love. Thick, fresh-tasting Greek yogurt cuts through the curd's sweetness, intensifying the lemon verbena flavour, while the honeycomb really enlivens the fragrant figs and rounds it all off quite stunningly.

MAKES 8

For the curd
60g (2oz / ¼ cup) crème fraîche
120g (4¼oz / ½ cup) lemon juice
70g (2½oz / ⅓ cup) golden caster (superfine) sugar
70g (2½oz / ¼ cup) honey
finely grated zest of 1 unwaxed lemon
10g (¼oz) dried lemon verbena leaves
3 eggs, plus 2 egg yolks
155g (5½oz / ⅔ cup / 1¼ sticks) soft unsalted butter

For the pastry (pie dough)
190g (6¾oz / ¾ cup / 1½ sticks) unsalted butter, cold and cut into cubes, plus more for the tins (pans)
250g (9oz / generous 2 cups) white spelt flour, plus more to dust
50g (1¾oz / ½ cup) ground almonds
½ tsp sea salt flakes
70g (2½oz / ⅓ cup) golden caster (superfine) sugar
finely grated zest of ½ unwaxed lemon
1 egg, plus 1 egg yolk to glaze (optional)
50g (1¾oz / ½ cup) jumbo oats

To serve
Greek-style yogurt
4 figs, halved
honeycomb

In a saucepan, warm the crème fraîche, lemon juice, sugar and honey, just bringing to a simmer to dissolve the sugar and honey. Turn off the heat, stir in the zest and verbena, cover and leave to infuse for 30 minutes to 1 hour.

Butter 8 x 10cm (4in) diameter, 2cm (¾in) deep tartlet tins (pans). Make the pastry by mixing together the flour, almonds, salt, sugar and lemon zest in a freestanding mixer. Add the cubes of butter and combine until the mix resembles crumbs. Add the egg and mix until it just comes together. Bring the pastry into a ball. Wrap in cling film (plastic wrap) and chill for 30 minutes.

In a medium saucepan, toast the oats until just becoming golden and smelling toasty. Divide them between the prepared tins (pans), spreading them evenly.

Lightly flour a piece of baking parchment, place the pastry on top, flour it, then roll it out under another sheet of baking parchment until 3mm (⅛in) thick. Cut out 8 circles to fit the tins. Press the pastry into the tins, trimming off excess. Chill for 30 minutes. Preheat the oven to 180°C/350°F/gas mark 4.

Strain the lemon verbena mix through a sieve, pushing it through to get all the flavour. Return to the heat and bring to the boil. In a bowl, mix the eggs and yolks. Pour over the hot lemon verbena syrup and mix. Return it to the pan over a low heat, mixing it with a whisk, then moving to a wooden spoon or silicone spatula. When it thickens enough to coat the back of the spoon or spatula, it is ready. (If you have a thermometer, heat it to 82°C / 180°F). Strain through a sieve into a bowl, leave to cool to body temperature, about 37°C (99°F), then blitz in the butter with a hand-held blender until smooth. Place cling film (plastic wrap) directly on the surface, and chill.

Put a circle of baking parchment in each shell, fill with baking beans and bake for 10 minutes. Remove the beans and parchment and bake for a further 8–10 minutes, or until golden brown. Leave to cool, then remove from the tins. At this point, you can brush the shells with egg yolk, baking for a few minutes to dry out. This is important if you are filling them in advance, less so if you are filling them just before serving. (Melted white chocolate brushed over the shells is another good option.) Fill each shell with the curd and top with yogurt, a half fig, honeycomb and a drizzle of honey from the comb.

The raw pastry, in a piece, or lining the shells, can be frozen for up to 1 month. Bake from frozen, adding a few more minutes to the baking time.

Honeyed semolina, pine nut and orange custard tarts

Inspired by a memorable dessert made by a very talented Greek chef, these tartlets are simple to make and totally sumptuous. First of all you taste the top layer of smooth custard with a little crunch from pine nuts; some of the semolina thickens the custard while the rest slowly sinks to the bottom of the tarts with the sultanas (golden raisins) and most of the zest to create a soft, cakey citrus layer, all encased in buttery, crunchy filo (phyllo) and infused with the sweetest honeyed orange blossom syrup

MAKES 6

For the semolina custard
30g (1oz / ¼ cup) pine nuts
200g (7oz / generous ¾ cup) whole milk
70g (2½oz / generous ¼ cup) double (heavy) cream
½ vanilla pod (bean), split lengthways, seeds scraped out
2 egg yolks
45g (1½oz / scant ¼ cup) runny honey
40g (1½oz / ¼ cup) semolina
finely grated zest of 1 orange
2 tsp orange blossom water
about 50g (1¾oz / 3½ tbsp) unsalted butter, melted, plus more for the tins (pans)
30 x 10cm (4in) squares of filo (phyllo) pastry, covered with a damp cloth
30g (1oz / ¼ cup) sultanas (golden raisins)

For the orange blossom syrup
50g (1¾oz / scant ¼ cup) honey
50g (1¾oz / scant ¼ cup) water
2–3 tsp orange blossom water

Preheat the oven to 180°C/350°F/gas mark 4.

Place a small frying pan (skillet) over a medium heat, tip in the pine nuts and toast them lightly. Tip them out on to a plate and leave to cool.

In a bowl, mix together all the custard ingredients from the milk to the orange blossom water.

Using a pastry brush, butter 6 muffin tins (pans) with a pastry brush and start layering in the filo (phyllo) sheets. You want 5 layers of filo (phyllo) in each tin (pan), each brushed with butter before adding the next. Give the custard a good whisk, then divide it between the shells using a ladle, or pour it into a jug (pitcher) first. Divide the sultanas (golden raisins) between the tarts, then top with the cooled pine nuts.

Bake for 10 minutes, then reduce the oven temperature to 150°C/300°F/gas mark 2 and bake for a further 10 minutes. You want the tarts to have a very slight wobble, but look firm and not liquid in the centre.

In a small saucepan, bring the honey and water to the boil over a medium heat and reduce it by about one-third. Remove from the heat and add the orange blossom water. Pour it over the tarts. Leave to sink in, then enjoy.

I love to serve these with fresh figs or berries, thick natural yogurt or ice cream and an extra drizzle of honey.

Black, red and white currant almond tarts

Who could resist these tarts of multicoloured currant jewels, emerging from a soft but slightly crunchy almond frangipane, encased in a wonderful, crumbly buckwheat and almond pastry shell and a layer of unctuous blackcurrant jam. As buckwheat is naturally gluten-free, it makes for an incredibly delicate and light pastry shell. As the seasons change, substitute the currants for other fruits, use different jams, or change the whole nuts in the frangipane: plums or caramelized apple slices work well with almonds, or try raspberries and figs with pistachios, and blueberries and blackberries with hazelnuts, as on the book cover.

MAKES 4

For the buckwheat and almond pastry (pie dough)

50g (1¾oz) virgin coconut oil or unsalted butter, plus more for the tins (pans)
75g (2¾oz / ¾ cup) ground almonds
75g (2¾oz / ½ cup) buckwheat flour, plus more to dust
30g (1oz / 1 tbsp) golden caster (superfine) or coconut sugar
10g (¼oz / 2 tsp) arrowroot (this helps to bind the ingredients in this gluten-free pastry)
¼ tsp sea salt flakes
finely grated zest of ½ unwaxed lemon

For the frangipane

90g (3¼oz / ½ cup) whole almonds
110g (4oz / ½ cup / 1 stick) unsalted butter, softened
80g (2¾oz / scant ½ cup) golden caster (superfine) or coconut sugar
½ tsp sea salt flakes
finely grated zest of ½ unwaxed lemon
2 medium eggs
90g (3¼oz / 1 cup) ground almonds
120g (4¼oz / scant ½ cup) blackcurrant jam
75g (2¾oz / ¾ cup) blackcurrants, fresh or frozen
75g (2¾oz / ¾ cup) redcurrants, fresh or frozen
75g (2¾oz / ¾ cup) whitecurrants, fresh or frozen
4 tbsp apricot jam, to glaze

Start by making the pastry. Oil or butter 4 x 10cm (4in) tart tins (pans). In a bowl, combine the dry ingredients from the almonds to the lemon zest. Melt the coconut oil or butter and mix it in, with 35g (1¼oz) cool water. The pastry will be soft. Roll it out to a circle between 2 pieces of baking parchment, dusted with a little flour, until 3mm (⅛in) thick. Take off the top piece of parchment and cut the pastry into 4 rounds to fit the tart tins (pans).

Using a cranked or step palette knife, lift the pastry, a piece at a time, off the parchment and use it to line the tins (pans). This is a gluten-free pastry so it will break, but do not worry, just piece it back together, making sure there are no gaps and each shell is well lined. If you need to re-roll the pastry or patch up any gaps, that's fine. Trim any excess, then rest the shells in the fridge for 10 minutes. Preheat the oven to 180°C/350°F/gas mark 4.

On a baking tray (sheet), bake the shells for about 10 minutes without baking beans. They will puff up a little and that's OK. Remove from the oven and leave on the tray (sheet) to cool slightly.

On a baking tray (sheet) lined with baking parchment, lightly toast the almonds in the oven for about 7 minutes. Leave to cool, then blitz in a food processor until fine, but with some texture. Cream the butter, sugar, salt and lemon zest until light and fluffy. Beat the eggs together. Combine the ground almonds with the toasted almonds. Gradually add the eggs to the butter mixture, alternating with the almonds, until the mix is smooth and homogenous.

Divide the blackcurrant jam between the tart shells and spread it out with the back of a spoon. Top with the frangipane, dividing it between the shells so that it comes just to the tops, then press a mixture of currants slightly into the frangipane. You will have some leftover frangipane; chill it for up to 1 week, freeze for up to 1 month, or bake it off in little cake tins (pans) or tart shells.

Bake the tarts for 10 minutes, then turn the tray (sheet) and bake for a further 5–8 minutes. They are ready when the edges of the frangipane are golden brown and the centres have a very slight wobble.

Leave to cool, then turn on to a serving plate. Warm the apricot jam gently with 1 tbsp water, to loosen its texture, then brush it over the tarts to glaze.

Cherry, pistachio and dark chocolate clafoutis with chocolate chip frozen yogurt

Clafoutis is gorgeous and simple, dense but light. Here I add cherries, macerated in a little kirsch, chunks of bitter chocolate and crunchy toasted pistachios. The fresh, sharp frozen yogurt, speckled with bitter chocolate chips and extra pistachios, is a lovely contrast to the rich chocolate, and provides that wonderful hot and cold contrast. A sumptuous end to a meal.

Brown teff flour has a subtle molasses flavour, so I like to add it here. It also keeps this gluten-free for those with allergies, however plain or wholegrain wheat flour will also be fine.

SERVES 10–12

For the frozen yogurt
40g (1½oz / scant ½ cup) pistachio nuts
40g (1½oz) 70% cocoa solids
  dark chocolate
475g (1lb 1oz / 2 cups) Greek-style
  yogurt
1 tsp vanilla extract
30g (1oz / 2 tbsp) maple syrup

For the cherries
400g (14oz / 2 cups) ripe cherries, the
  best you can find, pitted
2 tbsp light brown muscovado or
  coconut sugar
2 tbsp kirsch (optional)

For the batter
20g (¾oz / 1½ tbsp) unsalted butter, plus
  more for the dish
20g (¾oz / 4 tsp) light brown muscovado
  or coconut sugar, plus 1 tbsp
  for the dish
2 eggs
1 tsp vanilla extract
2 tbsp brown teff flour (see recipe
  introduction)
50g (1¾oz / scant ¼ cup) whole milk
100g (3½oz / generous ⅓ cup) double
  (heavy) cream
pinch of sea salt flakes
60g (2oz) 70% cocoa solids
  dark chocolate
40g (1½oz / scant ½ cup) pistachio nuts,
  plus more, chopped, to serve

Start with the frozen yogurt. Roughly chop the pistachios in a food processor. Chop the chocolate with a knife into smaller-than-pea-sized pieces. Place them both in a bowl and stir in the rest of the ingredients. Place in a freezable dish, cover and put in the freezer.

Mix together the cherries, sugar and kirsch, if using, in a bowl. Set aside for the fruit to macerate.

Preheat the oven to 180°C/350°F/gas mark 4. Butter a 23cm (9in) diameter baking dish and sprinkle with 1 tbsp sugar. Shake the sugar around the dish so that it is evenly coated, then tip out any excess.

Heat the butter in a small pan until it turns a pale hazelnut colour (this is called a *beurre noisette*). Do not allow the butter to burn, or it will become bitter. Remove the pan from the heat and set aside.

In a large bowl, whisk together the eggs, sugar and vanilla until creamy. Add the flour, whisk until smooth, then slowly incorporate the milk, cream, salt and *beurre noisette*.

Roughly chop the chocolate and the pistachios. You want quite good chunks of chocolate, a bit smaller than a £1 coin; just roughly halve the pistachios. Mix them into the batter with the macerated cherries and their juices. Pour into the prepared baking dish.

Bake in the oven for 20 minutes, then rotate the dish and bake for a further 10 minutes, or until the top is slightly domed and the blade of a knife inserted in the middle comes out clean (except for smears of melty chocolate). Serve warm, with scoops of frozen yogurt and a sprinkling of chopped pistachios. If the frozen yogurt has been in the freezer for a little while, take it out for 5–10 minutes before serving, to soften.

Dark chocolate mousse, prune and brandy tart with rye cocoa pastry

A most sublime pudding: a gorgeous, crumbling malty flavoured cocoa and wholegrain rye pastry (pie crust) base, juicy sweet prunes and a rich, bitter chocolate mousse-like filling. Thank you Tal and Rebecca for inspiring the mousse filling, and to Jeremy Lee for a chocolate and prune creation I tasted at Quo Vadis in London and have never forgotten. This makes just the right amount of pastry (dough), so there is no waste.

SERVES 12–14

For the pastry (pie dough)
90g (3¼oz / ⅓ cup / ¾ stick) cold unsalted butter, cubed, plus more for the tin (pan)
80g (2¾oz / generous ½ cup) wholegrain wheat flour
80g (2¾oz / generous ½ cup) rye flour
20g (¾oz / ¼ cup) cocoa powder, plus more to dust (optional)
40g (1½oz / scant ¼ cup) light brown muscovado or coconut sugar
½ tsp sea salt flakes
2 egg yolks, plus 1 egg yolk, to glaze
1 tsp vanilla extract

For the prune filling
300g (10½oz / 2⅓ cups) good-quality pitted prunes (figs work well, too)
90g (3¼oz / ⅓ cup) orange juice (about 1 orange), plus zest of ½ orange, pared with a vegetable peeler or small knife
⅓ vanilla pod (bean), split lengthways, seeds scraped out
90g (3¼oz / ⅓ cup) brandy

For the chocolate filling
180g (6oz) 70% cocoa solids dark chocolate
115g (4oz / ½ cup / 1 stick) unsalted butter
3 eggs, plus 2 egg yolks
30g (1oz / 2 tbsp) light brown muscovado or coconut sugar

Filling variation: Replace the prunes with figs and, after spreading over the tart shell, top with a layer of cooked quince slices (see page 172), then the chocolate filling.

Butter a 28cm (11in) loose-bottomed tart tin (pan). In a freestanding mixer fitted with a paddle, mix the flours, cocoa, sugar and salt. Add the butter and mix until it resembles crumbs. Add the 2 egg yolks and vanilla and process until it comes together. Flatten out to a 2.5cm- (1in-) thick circle on a piece of baking parchment. Roll out the pastry between 2 pieces of baking parchment until it is 3mm (⅛in) thick. It is quite dry, so dusting with flour shouldn't be necessary. Line the tin (pan), trim the edges and chill for 30 minutes.

Preheat the oven to 180°C/350°F/gas mark 4. In a saucepan, cook the prunes with the orange juice, zest and vanilla. Add 60g (2oz / ¼ cup) of the brandy and simmer to plump up the prunes; most of the liquid should be absorbed. Remove from the heat, remove the zest and transfer to a food processor. Process with the remaining 30g (1oz / 1 tbsp) brandy to form a paste.

Line the pastry shell with baking parchment and baking beans. Bake for 10 minutes. Remove the beans and parchment and bake for 10 minutes. Brush with egg yolk and bake to dry out for 1–2 minutes. Leave to cool. Spread the prunes over. Reduce the oven temperature to 150°C/300°F/gas mark 2.

For the chocolate filling, melt the chocolate and butter in a heatproof bowl over a saucepan of simmering water (make sure the bowl does not touch the water). With an electric whisk, or in a freestanding mixer fitted with a whisk, whisk the eggs, yolks and sugar until light and forming ribbons when you lift up the whisk. Lightly whisk one-third of the egg mixture into the chocolate mix, then fold in the next one-third with a spatula, then the final one-third, scooping up the mix from the bottom so everything is combined. Pour over the prunes and bake for 10 minutes, until just firm but with a wobble. Leave in the tin (pan) for 30 minutes, or until firm. Dust with cocoa powder, if you like, and serve with crème fraîche, thick yogurt or ice cream. Keep leftovers in the fridge for up to 5 days. The raw pastry will freeze for 1 month.

Variations: Make great chocolate biscuits (cookies) with the pastry. Roll and cut into 4cm (1½in) shapes and bake for 10 minutes at 180°C/350°F/gas mark 4.

For a ganache filling, semi-melt 300g (10½oz) 85% cocoa solids dark chocolate, as above. Add 300g (10½oz / 1¼ cups) boiling water or cream and mix lightly. Pour into the baked shell and chill for 30 minutes. Sprinkle with sea salt flakes and serve.

Crema Catalana bread and butter pudding with sherry figs

I made crema Catalana for the first time when I took my pâtisserie scholarship. It was about a year ago that those wonderful flavours of citrus and cinnamon came back to me, when I tasted the most delicious Spanish custard gelato from Poco Gelato, a gorgeous gelateria in Essex that uses free-range Guernsey milk and seasonal fruits, giving me the idea for this recipe. (You can see Joe's pastel-pretty gelato on page 94, thank you, Joe!) The layers of oozing, spiced and fragrant custard and juicy figs are quite irresistible, and the figs on top caramelize and become chewier, which adds a delectable texture. Cinnamon sticks alone are also fine, but I love the extra zings of flavour from the anise and fennel, too. Do use soft, plump dried figs, though you could soak them in warm water or tea for 10 minutes if they are very dry.

SERVES 8–10

For the figs
300g (10½oz / 2½ cups) soft dried figs, stalks removed
200g (7oz / generous ¾ cup) Pedro Ximénez, or other sweet sherry
100g (3½oz / generous ⅓ cup) water
3 black cardamom pods
3 star anise
½ vanilla pod (bean), split lengthways, seeds scraped out

For the pudding
unsalted butter for the bread, plus more for the dish
800g (1lb 12oz / 3⅓ cups) whole milk
200g (7oz / generous ¾ cup) double (heavy) cream
2 cinnamon sticks
5 pared strips of unwaxed lemon zest
5 pared strips of orange zest
5 star anise (optional)
2 tsp fennel seeds (optional)
½ vanilla pod (bean), split lengthways, seeds scraped out
10 egg yolks
180g (6oz / ½ cup) runny honey
350g (12oz) sourdough bread (5–6 large slices), crusts cut off if you like (I prefer them with the crusts on)
light brown muscovado or coconut sugar, to sprinkle

Start by preparing the figs. Roughly chop them and place them in a small-ish saucepan with the rest of the fig ingredients, including the empty vanilla pod (bean). Bring to the boil, then reduce the heat slightly to a simmer and reduce the liquid by about half, leaving a lovely syrup. Remove from the heat and set aside. The figs should be plump.

Butter a 30 x 20 x 6cm (12 x 8 x 2½in) square ovenproof dish, or equivalent. Make the custard. Bring the milk and cream just to the boil with all the ingredients from the cinnamon sticks to the vanilla, including the empty vanilla pod (bean). When it's all just reached boiling point, turn off the heat and leave to infuse for 30 minutes, covered with cling film (plastic wrap). Put the egg yolks in a large bowl and add the honey. Strain the milk and spice mix over the egg yolks and honey and whisk to combine.

Butter the slices of bread on both sides. Start to layer up the pudding by covering the bottom of the prepared dish with buttered slices of bread, cutting them to fit if necessary. Add about two-thirds of the figs along with all their syrup. Top with the rest of the bread and then pour over the custard, topping with the remaining figs, slotting them into any gaps in the bread. You don't want too many straight on top of the last layer of bread, or they will burn. Let the custard sink in for 30 minutes. (If you have any leftover custard, just warm it over a low heat and serve with the pudding.)

Preheat the oven to 160°C/325°F/gas mark 3. Sprinkle the top of the pudding with a handful of light brown muscovado or coconut sugar and bake for about 30 minutes, or until the custard has just set and the top is golden brown. Serve warm from the oven, with extra cream or ice cream.

Variation: Leave out the bread and make custard pots, with or without the figs, in individual ramekins. Bake the mixture in an oven preheated to 120°C/250°F/ gas mark ½ until firm but with a little wobble (this could take 20–30 minutes, depending on the size of the ramekins). The pudding or custard pots are both lovely with plumped raisins; chopped candied orange peel makes a great addition, too.

Plum, blackberry and blueberry crumble with rosemary and lemon syrup

I love my crumbles very fruity and juicy, but with a good amount of topping, and this ticks all those boxes! Both blackberries and blueberries have quite subtle flavours, but the combination with sweet plums, aromatic rosemary and sharp lemon really lifts them up. The brown sugar in the crumble adds depth and robustness, standing up to – and complementing – the rosemary very well. Serve with natural yogurt, crème fraîche or ice cream for a wonderful late summer or early autumn (fall) dessert.

SERVES 8–10

For the filling

80g (2¾oz / scant ½ cup) light brown muscovado or coconut sugar
pared zest of 1 unwaxed lemon
50g (1¾oz / scant ¼ cup) lemon juice
4 small sprigs of rosemary (12g / ¼oz)
60g (2oz / ¼ cup) water
700g (1lb 9oz) firm-ish ripe plums (pitted weight), pitted and halved (I use orange-yellow plums for this)
250g (9oz / 2 cups) blackberries, fresh or frozen
250g (9oz / 2 cups) blueberries, fresh or frozen

For the topping

100g (3½oz / scant 1 cup) wholegrain spelt or wheat flour
100g (3½oz / 1 cup) rolled or jumbo oats, or a mixture
100g (3½oz / 1 cup) ground almonds
80g (2¾oz / scant ½ cup) light brown muscovado or coconut sugar
150g (5½oz / ⅔ cup / 1¼ sticks) chilled unsalted butter, cubed, or virgin coconut oil (butter creates a crunchier crumble)

Preheat the oven to 180°C/350°F/gas mark 4.

In a medium-large saucepan, bring the sugar, lemon zest and juice and rosemary to the boil with the water. Add the plum halves, reduce the heat and cover with a lid for 10 minutes, stirring now and again. Now turn off the heat, lightly mix in the blackberries and blueberries and set aside.

In a freestanding mixer fitted with a paddle, by hand, or with a food processor, combine the flour, oats, ground almonds and sugar. Add the butter or coconut oil and process until the mix resembles crumbs.

Remove the rosemary and lemon zest from the cooked plums and berries (although I quite like to leave the lemon zest in, it's up to you). Pour the fruits into an ovenproof dish: using a shallow, longer dish will allow for a crumblier top; a taller dish will mean that part of the crumble absorbs the juice and becomes soft… so choose your crumble preference! Spread the crumble over the top and bake for 30 minutes, until the top is golden brown and the fruit juices are bubbling up around the edges. Serve hot.

Keep any leftovers in the fridge for at least 5 days, there's nothing better than leftover crumble! The raw crumble mix can be frozen in freezer bags for at least 1 month.

Rye, apple and sultana (golden raisin) pudding-cake with hazelnut crumble top and maple custard

The juices from fresh apples merge into this wholesome rye sponge, creating a soft and comforting after dinner-type cake with the contrasting crunchy crumble finishing it all off wonderfully. Serve warm from the oven for tea, or after supper with custard, and everyone will be happy!

SERVES 8–10

For the crumble
35g (1¼oz / ¼ cup) rye flour
65g (2¼oz / scant ½ cup) hazelnuts, whole with skins, or blanched
pinch of sea salt flakes
½ tbsp light brown muscovado or coconut sugar, plus more for the top
30g (1oz / 2 tbsp) cold unsalted butter, cubed

For the cake
120g (4¼oz / ½ cup / 1⅛ sticks) unsalted butter, softened, plus more for the tin (pan)
2 dessert apples such as Granny Smith or Cox, or use 1 of each (total weight 300g / 10½oz), peeled, cored, quartered and cut into 1–2cm (½–¾in) chunks; you want to get about 200g (7oz) apple chunks
60g (2oz / ⅓ cup) sultanas (golden raisins)
finely grated zest of 1 unwaxed lemon, plus 2 tsp lemon juice
60g (2oz / generous ¼ cup) light brown muscovado or coconut sugar
120g (4¼oz) Apple purée (see page 102)
1 tsp vanilla extract
110g (4oz / ¾ cup) rye flour, plus 10g (¼oz / 2tsp) more for the apples
1 scant tsp ground cinnamon
pinch of sea salt flakes
1½ tsp baking powder
2 eggs

For the maple custard
125g (4½oz / ½ cup) whole milk
125g (4½oz / ½ cup) double (heavy) cream
½ vanilla pod (bean), split lengthways, seeds scraped out
4 egg yolks, about 80g (2¾oz)
45g (1¾oz / scant ¼ cup) maple syrup

Preheat the oven to 180°C/350°F/gas mark 4. Butter the sides and base of an 18 x 11 x 8cm (7 x 4½ x 3in) loaf tin (pan), or an equivalent suitable size, and line the base with baking parchment.

For the crumble, place the flour, hazelnuts, salt and sugar in a food processor and process until the nuts are in pieces slightly smaller than peas, so you still have some texture. Add the butter and blend until it resembles crumbs. Set aside somewhere cool. In a bowl, combine the apple chunks and sultanas (golden raisins) and toss with the 2 tsp of lemon juice. Set aside.

Whisk together the butter, sugar, Apple purée and vanilla in a freestanding mixer or with an electric whisk until combined. Don't worry if the mix looks a little split. Mix together the dry ingredients from the flour to the baking powder. While whisking the butter mixture, add one-third of the dry ingredients, then the lemon zest and 1 egg, another one-third of the dry ingredients, the second egg, then the remaining dry ingredients. Scrape the batter from the edges of the bowl and whisk once more until smooth.

Toss the prepared apples and sultanas (golden raisins) with the remaining 10g (¼oz / 2 tsp) flour and fold them into the cake mix. Pour into the prepared tin (pan), smooth it out with a knife, then cover with the crumble and a sprinkling of sugar. Press the crumble well into the mix and bake for 20 minutes, then rotate the tin (pan), reduce the oven temperature to 170°C/340°F/gas mark 3½ and bake for a further 20 minutes. Finally, turn the tin (pan) once more, reduce the oven temperature to 160°C/325°F/gas mark 3 and bake for a final 20 minutes, until the top is dark golden and a skewer inserted into the centre comes out clean. Leave to cool slightly.

Meanwhile, make the custard. Heat the milk and cream with the vanilla seeds. Place the yolks and maple syrup in a bowl. When the milk is just about to boil, pour over the egg yolks and maple syrup, whisking, then return the mix to the saucepan and place over a medium-low heat. Stir with a wooden spoon until the custard coats the back of a spoon and a finger passed through it leaves a mark. Or measure it with a thermometer; it should be 82°C (180°F) when cooked. Pass through a sieve and transfer to a jug (pitcher).

Run a knife around the edge of the loaf tin (pan), demould the cake and serve warm with the custard, sprinkling over any crumble that has fallen off. Any remaining cake will keep in the fridge for up to 5 days. Warm it up gently before serving.

Prune, honey, buckwheat and walnut crumble cheesecake

This recipe was inspired by a Polish cheesecake I once read about. Instead of using biscuits (cookies) in the base, I make my own crumble with buckwheat flour and walnuts: their nutty, buttery notes really complement the richly flavoured prunes. I urge you to buy the best-quality, juiciest prunes you can find to create the most sumptuous prune layer possible. The crunch of the base, the soft plump prunes and the creamy filling with its lingering notes of fragrant honey are quite delightful, with a good amount of lemon juice adding a balancing freshness.

SERVES 14–16

For the base
70g (2½oz / ⅓ cup / ⅔ stick) cold
   unsalted butter, cubed, plus 1 tsp,
   plus more for the tin (pan)
75g (2¾oz / ½ cup) buckwheat flour
150g (5½oz / 1½ cups) walnuts
good pinch of sea salt flakes
30g (1oz / 2 tbsp) light brown muscovado
   or coconut sugar
good pinch of ground nutmeg

For the prune filling
350g (12oz / 2⅔ cups) prunes
finely grated zest of 1 unwaxed lemon,
   plus 60g (2oz / ¼ cup) lemon juice
1 cinnamon stick
2 bay leaves
35g (1¼oz / heaping 2 tbsp) honey

For the cheesecake filling
500g (1lb 2oz / 2¼ cups) cream cheese,
   at room temperature
800g (1lb 12oz / 3½ cups) mascarpone
   cheese
260g (9½oz / ¾ cup) runny honey
50g (1¾oz / ¼ cup) golden caster
   (superfine) sugar
finely grated zest of 2¼ unwaxed lemons,
   plus 80g (2¾oz / ⅓ cup) lemon juice
8 medium eggs, lightly beaten
seeds from 1 vanilla pod (bean)
1 tsp vanilla extract
pinch of sea salt flakes

Preheat the oven to 180°C/350°F/gas mark 4. Line a baking tray (sheet) with baking parchment. Butter the base and sides of a 23cm (9in) loose-bottomed cake tin (pan) and line the base and sides with baking parchment, allowing a collar above the edges of the tin (pan), for the cheesecake to rise.

Start by making the base. Process all the dry ingredients until fine but with some texture of the walnuts remaining. Add the butter and process once more until the mix resembles crumbs. Turn on to the prepared tray (sheet) and bake for 10 minutes, then stir and bake for a further 2 minutes, or until golden brown. Leave to cool. Once cool, return to the food processor, add the remaining 1 tsp butter and process until it comes together. Turn out into the prepared tin (pan), press it in firmly and evenly, and freeze for 30 minutes.

Bring all the ingredients for the prune filling to the boil in a small saucepan, then reduce the heat and simmer for 5 minutes, until the juice reduces; there should be a little remaining. Remove the cinnamon stick and bay leaves and pour over the chilled base, spreading the prunes out evenly with the back of a spoon or a cranked or step palette knife. Refrigerate.

Preheat the oven to 160°C/325°F/gas mark 3. By hand, or using a freestanding mixer, whisk together the cream cheese, mascarpone, honey and sugar until smooth. Add the remaining ingredients and whisk until smooth. Pour over the prune layer and bake for 2 hours. The top should be golden brown and the centre should have a little wobble. Leave to cool completely.

This will keep for about 1 week in the fridge, in fact, it gets better with age! You can also freeze the cooked crumble base for at least 1 month.

Variation: If you want, try 325g (11oz) of Wholegrain oat bran malty biscuits (cookies) (see page 98) for the base, instead of the mixture above. Bake them as described, leave to cool, then process in a food processor with the 1 tsp of butter, press into the prepared tin (pan) and proceed as in the recipe above.

Baked bananas with lime and coconut cream and cocoa nib tuile

This is fun, simple and delicious, with the sweetness of the bananas beautifully balanced out by the zingy-fresh lime and coconut cream and the bitter cocoa nib tuile. The cream is light, the banana soft, oozing in an orange syrup spiked with a little rum, while the tuile adds that extra snap and crunch. It's a great one to make after all the meat, fish and vegetables have come off the barbecue: just put the bananas on the grill and wait for them to turn black and squidgy.

SERVES 5

For the tuille
55g (2oz / ¼ cup) light brown muscovado or coconut sugar
50g (1¾oz) unsalted butter
20g (¾oz / 4 tsp) maple syrup
10g (¼oz / 2 tsp) whole milk
50g (1¾oz / scant ½ cup) cocoa nibs

For the bananas
5 medium bananas
120g (4¼oz / ½ cup) orange juice
15g (½oz / 1 tbsp) lime juice
2 tsp light brown muscovado or coconut sugar
1 tsp rum, or more to taste

For the cream
2 x 160g cans of coconut cream
100g (3½oz / generous ⅓ cup) natural coconut yogurt
1 tsp maple syrup, or golden icing (confectioners') sugar, or to taste
finely grated zest of 1 lime, plus more to serve (optional), plus 1 tsp lime juice
a few handfuls of flaked coconut, toasted (see page 106), to serve (optional)

Preheat the oven to 180°C/350°F/gas mark 4. Line a baking tray (sheet) with a silicone mat or baking parchment.

Start by making the tuille. In a saucepan set over a medium heat, whisk together the sugar, butter, maple syrup and milk and bring to the boil. Remove from the heat, add the cocoa nibs and stir in. Pour on to the prepared tray (sheet), spread out a little with a palette knife and bake for 10 minutes. There will be a few bubbles still bubbling, but most should have stopped. Leave to cool completely on the tray (sheet).

Increase the oven temperature to 200°C/400°F/gas mark 6. Place the bananas, still in their skins, in the oven on a tray (sheet). Cook for 30 minutes, turning over halfway, until the skins have blackened and they feel soft and squidgy. Boil together the orange and lime juices and sugar to a sweet syrup: it will take 2 minutes on a high boil. Add the rum and remove from the heat.

Make the cream by whisking together all the ingredients, except the flaked coconut, until smooth. Taste for sweetness and add more syrup or sugar if you like.

To serve, remove the bananas from their skins into bowls or on to plates. Add spoonfuls of cream, pour over the rum syrup and finish with a bit of tuile, scattering with more lime zest and some flaked coconut, if you like. Keep any remaining cream in the fridge for about 5 days and any remaining tuile in a dry place in an airtight container for at least 1 week.

You can also make the tuille, spread it out over the baking parchment and freeze raw for at least 1 month. Bake the sheet from frozen, adding 2 minutes to the baking time.

Chocolate and chestnut ricotta soufflés

Chocolate and chestnut, like chocolate and orange, chocolate and mint and so many more bitter cocoa combinations, are meant to be together. Unlike a traditional sweet soufflé mix, which involves a pastry cream foundation, these have a velvety smooth ricotta base. This creates a gorgeously light souffléd mix that balances out the luscious bursting centre of rich, melting chocolate and *marrons glacés*. Serve with chestnut or vanilla ice cream and your guests will be silenced by satisfaction!

You can always leave out the *marrons glacés*, if you would prefer a plain chocolate soufflé; the recipe will still work just as well, though perhaps won't be quite as festive.

MAKES 3 SMALL SOUFFLÉS

soft unsalted butter, for the ramekins
15g (½oz / 1 tbsp) cocoa powder,
  plus 2 tsp for the ramekins
45g (1¾oz / ¼ cup) light brown
  muscovado or coconut sugar,
  plus 2 tsp for the ramekins
3 x 5g (⅛oz) lumps of 70–85% cocoa
  solids dark chocolate
3 *marrons glacés*, halved
135g (4¾oz / ⅔ cup) ricotta
2 eggs, separated
golden icing (confectioners') sugar, to
  dust (optional)

Preheat the oven to 180°C/350°F/gas mark 4 and place a baking tray (sheet) inside to heat up.

Butter 3 ceramic ramekins using a pastry brush, brushing vertically up the sides of the ramekins, as if to help the soufflé rise up. Combine the extra teaspoons of cocoa powder and sugar and coat the bottom and sides of the ramekins with this, tapping out any excess. Set aside.

Sandwich each piece or pieces of chocolate (if they've broken more) between 2 halves of a marron glacé.

Fill an ovenproof and flameproof roasting tin (pan), large enough to fit all the ramekins in, with water 2–3cm (¾–1¼in) deep, and put over a medium-high heat until it comes to the boil.

Meanwhile, combine the ricotta, cocoa powder and egg yolks. Separately whisk the egg whites until light and fluffy, then add the muscovado sugar and whisk a little more until just combined. Fold the whisked whites carefully into the ricotta base. Divide the mix between the 3 ramekins. Push the chocolate-filled chestnuts into the centre of each and down to the bottom. Using a palette knife, or a regular knife, run over the top of each soufflé so it has a smooth top, then sweep around the edge of each ramekin with your thumb so that you can just see the rim.

Turn the boiling water off under the roasting tin (pan), place the soufflés in it so that the water comes 2–3cm (¾–1¼in) up the sides of each ramekin, and place on the hot tray in the middle of the oven. Bake for 12–15 minutes, or until risen with a slight wobble, and serve immediately, dusted with icing (confectioners') sugar, if you like.

Brown sugar pecan meringues with quince and marsala cream

Served with whipped cream and seasonal fruit, meringues are a delicious and timeless classic. I really enjoy making mine with brown sugar, as it caramelizes around the crunchy pecan nuts and adds a light, treacly depth which is particularly good with autumn (fall) and winter fruits. Some describe quince as in between an apple and a pear, but they have a much more fragrant, completely unique sweetness complemented so well here by the vanilla and apricot notes in the Marsala cream, and the rich pecans. With a crunch from the meringues, a softness from the tender quince and smoothness from the creamy clouds of whipped cream, it's a really wonderful dessert.

Keep the leftover egg yolks in the fridge (see page 14) and use them for mayonnaise, pastry or custard.

SERVES 8

For the meringues
3 egg whites
90g (3¼oz / scant ½ cup) light brown muscovado sugar
90g (3¼oz / ⅔ cup) golden icing (confectioners') sugar
70g (2½oz / ¾ cup) pecan nuts

For the quince
4 quince, about 1kg (2lb 4oz) in total, peeled, cored, each cut into about 12 x 1cm (½in) slices
½ vanilla pod (bean), split lengthways, seeds scraped out
pared zest and juice of 1 orange
1 cinnamon stick
100g (3½oz / ½ cup) light brown muscovado or coconut sugar

For the cream
400g (14oz / 1¾ cups) double (heavy) cream
1–2 tbsp Marsala, or to taste (optional)

Preheat the oven to 100°C/225°F/gas mark ¼ and line a baking tray (sheet) with baking parchment.

In a freestanding mixer fitted with a whisk, or with an electric hand whisk, whisk the egg whites until light and fluffy, then add the light brown sugar and half the golden icing (confectioners') sugar and whisk until the mixture holds stiff peaks. Sift over the remaining icing (confectioners') sugar, then roughly break in 40g (1½oz / scant ½ cup) of the pecans and fold the icing (confectioners') sugar and pecans into the meringue until just combined.

Using large spoons, spoon out 8 meringues on to the prepared tray (sheet), scooping the mix off using another spoon and being careful not to knock them. Crumble over the remaining pecans, pressing them a little to stick them to the meringues, and bake for 1 hour, or until they peel off the baking parchment and sound hollow when tapped on the bottom. Leave to cool.

For the quince, place all the ingredients in a saucepan over a medium heat. When the orange juice and sugar comes to the boil, cover, reduce the heat and cook for 15–20 minutes, until soft. You should be able to pierce a piece of quince all the way through with a sharp knife, but don't take it too far as you don't want to pulverize them.

Whip the cream to soft peaks, being careful not to overwhip, then fold in the Marsala. Refrigerate until serving.

Serve the meringues with the cream and quince. Keep any remaining meringues in an airtight container in a dry place for at least 2 weeks.

Variation: Do play around with the nuts, or you could swirl some cocoa powder into the meringues with the final half of the golden icing (confectioners') sugar, if you like.

Try the meringues with Plum compote (see page 30), baked apples (see page 26), red wine-poached pears (see page 80) or rhubarb compote.

index

stockists

Suffolk producers I love:
www.fenfarmdairy.co.uk
www.hillfarmoils.com
www.hodmedods.co.uk
www.maplefarmkelsale.co.uk
www.pumpstreetbakery.com

For flours:
www.dovesfarm.co.uk
www.flour.co.uk
www.gilchesters.com
www.sharphampark.com

For gluten-free flours:
in the UK, www.shipton-mill.com
in the USA, www.bobsredmill.com

And a few more things, available online, in supermarkets and health food shops:

www.biona.co.uk
Coconut products, date syrup, apple cider vinegar and brown rice pasta

www.meridian.co.uk
Maple syrup, molasses, barley malt extract and nut butters

www.realfoodsource.com
Coconut products and dry produce such as nuts, seeds and nut butters

www.rudehealth.com
Sprouted wheat, buckwheat and spelt flours and plant-based milks

www.stdalfour.co.uk
No added cane sugar fruit preserves

www.steenbergs.co.uk
Pure extracts and flower waters

For fresh produce:
Seek out your nearest farmers' markets and producers and buy local when you can

acknowledgements

First of all, thank you, reader, for buying this book. To create recipes with ingredients that I truly love – and to be able to share them with you all and imagine you cooking them in your kitchens – brings me so much joy. I am so grateful to you, Jacqui, for giving me the opportunity to do it again. Thank you and Fritha for allowing it to happen. Thank you, Rachel, for always listening to me, the mad, perfectionist pastry chef that I am, and for your beautiful design work. Lucy, thank you for understanding how I bake, keeping my voice and editing so seamlessly. Linda, thank you for letting me come along with you to the prop houses and for indulging (and controlling!) my desire for as much colour and pattern as possible. Your reassurance and calm helped me so much in the run-up to the shoots. And from one kind soul to another, Philippa. No matter how clichéd it sounds, you have made my vision come to life with each photo in this book. I am forever indebted to you for the love, dedication, patience and many extra hours that you put in; you are a shining star. Thank you, Philippa, and those awesome assistants of yours, Stephanie and KJ. We made this book as a team, thank you all.

Heather, thank you for encouraging me to write my second book and for getting the ball rolling. I feel incredibly lucky to have you as an agent and friend who I can turn to under any circumstances. I do not know what I would have done without you and your wise and wonderful Cara. Thank you both for always being there.

Thank you to those who tested recipes, friends and past students. Felicity, Fiona, Joey, Clare, Dara, Kate, Ceri, Carri, Jo, Louise and everyone who volunteered on social media. It was so useful to get your feedback, thank you. Nena, you tested my recipes with diligence and dedication and with you there on the first two days of the shoot it was all so much better. Thank you.

To all my guinea pigs who put up with endless questions, even after you'd told me what you thought, which was mainly lots of kind and positive things! And to my Potluck Princesses and Boris for eating bread-and-butter (and rice) pudding on the hottest day of the year and for always inspiring my culinary adventures. Here's to many more magical meals together!

Tal, thank goodness it was you! You are my mentor and I would not be where I am today without you having taken a chance on me, even after seeing disastrous consequences as you witnessed me using a piping bag for the first time! Thank you, Tal and Rebecca. You have both become true friends and your continuing support for my career means the world to me. Alan, Fabian, Pascal, Attila, Tommaso, Olivia, Sophie and all The Lanesborough team, the best team ever! Working with you all inspired me to take this path in my career, thank you so much! Massimiliano and Marco, you're both completely crazy, but working with you taught me so much and made me stronger. *Grazie per tutto…* and for inspiring the soufflés on page 170. Leti, Leo, Takeru, Will and Andrea, our time working together was cut short, but I loved every moment of it and I'm so grateful that we had it. Thank you, Francesco, for being so kind, always.

Thank you to customers, friends and family who support my natural baking back at home in Suffolk. To all the producers and enterprises who encourage and inspire my work.

The food community in London is such a buzzing and friendly world that I am so happy and grateful to be a part of. The wealth of energetic chefs, cooks, food writers and authors who live in this city constantly inspire me. Thank you all.

Thank you Anna and Amy for your kind words and enthusiasm for how I bake. Meera, I'm so happy we are neighbours. Thank you for the props you lent me and for your friendship and support. Thank you, Rosemary and Minny, for the figs, apples and blue table. Thank you, Caroline, for your jewel-like currants, Shirleen for your flowers, and Keith for the Stella cherries. Kylee, I know your secret ingredient, it's love! Thank you for your divine jam on page 63 and Elisabetta for your *formaggi* that inspired many a recipe. Laurie, Clare, Sam, Sumayya and Polly, thank you for keeping me sane.

To my sister, Miranda, and my brother, Rupert. Thank you for always being there for me, for putting up with me and for winding me up when I take life too seriously. Granny, I loved baking for you and you inspired me so much. David, I miss you terribly but wearing your ring gives me strength every day. Daddy, you keep me calm, my head screwed on and my feet on the ground. Mummy, you taught me to see colour, flowers, nature and beauty and words cannot describe how much being by my side during the photo shoots meant to me. Thank you both. You let me follow my heart. This book is for you.

Henrietta Inman is the author of *Clean Cakes*. A skilled pastry chef and cookery teacher, she has worked in award-winning kitchens including The Lanesborough Hotel and the Michelin-starred Apsleys. She now lives and works in London and Suffolk where she takes private commissions and bespoke orders, holds cookery classes and baking demonstrations and does food consultancy, supper clubs and events.